Contents

List of Figures

List of Tables

List of Abbreviations

AHA	Area Health Authority
ATO	Area Team of Officers
CHC	Community Health Council
DA	District Administrator
DGH	District General Hospital
DGM	District General Manager
DHA	District Health Authority
DHSS	Department of Health and Social Security
DMC	District Medical Committee
DMT	District Management Team
DNS	Director of Nursing Services
GP	General Practitioner
HAS	Health Advisory Service
HCPT	Health Care Planning Team
HMC	Hospital Management Committee
MIND	National Association for Mental Health
MOH	Medical Officer of Health
NHS	National Health Service
NHSTA	National Health Service Training Authority
PIs	Performance Indicators
RAWP	Resource Allocation Working Party
RGM	Regional General Manager
RHA	Regional Health Authority
RHB	Regional Health Board
SCM	Senior Physician in Community Medicine
UGM	Unit General Manager

Acknowledgements

I am especially grateful to:

Rosemary Stewart, now Emeritus Fellow at Templeton College, for employing me as a researcher, to work on a most fascinating research project.

Ivan Waddington, the supervisor of my PhD thesis, who has been an unfailing and unflagging mentor, friend, intellectual critic and eagle-eyed copy-editor.

Ray Fitzpatrick for his encouragement and invaluable advice on research and teaching medical sociology.

Finally, full and proper thanks have to go to Val Martin for her considerate friendship, support and technical assistance throughout, and far beyond the call of duty.

SUE DOPSON

Preface

The central focus of this book is managing change in the National Health Service (NHS). In particular it considers the introduction of general management into the NHS – its third major reorganization and one based on the recommendations of a team of businessmen led by Sir Roy Griffiths, then managing director and deputy chairman of Sainsbury foodstores. More than previous reorganizations of the NHS in 1974 and 1982, the Griffiths changes were a conscious attempt to move away from a 'boxes and charts' approach to organizational change towards one which sought to disturb organizational processes and ultimately to change the beliefs and values of NHS actors.

The book attempts to illuminate the implications of what was viewed as a significant change in the way the NHS was managed, in three ways. Firstly it reviews the existing empirical work on health service management and considers what can be learnt about the difficulties of introducing change in the NHS. Secondly it reports fieldwork data from 20 NHS districts which explored the actions and priorities of 20 newly appointed DGMs with a variety of different occupational backgrounds as they sought to implement the agenda for change spelt out in the Griffiths Report. The book reports a significant gap between the aspirations of the Griffiths Report and what the introduction of general management was able to deliver, and a number of unintended consequences. Thirdly the book draws on the work of Norbert Elias, known as figurational or process sociology, in an attempt to illuminate the fieldwork data further. Elias is not a sociologist one associates with the study of the NHS, or indeed the management of change, yet it is argued that his writings offer much to those wishing to explore organizational and management issues in the NHS.

SUE DOPSON

1 Introduction

This book's central object is to address some of the more theoretical issues involved in the analysis of what might be called 'managed social change', that is to say, change which has been deliberately initiated with the specific objective of achieving some formally stated policy goal. There are many theories that can assist in understanding issues surrounding 'managed social change' (many are helpfully reviewed in Pettigrew *et al.*'s book *Shaping Strategic Change*, 1992). It is suggested in this book that the process-sociological approach developed by Norbert Elias, and in particular Elias's game models, may be another useful approach for those studying health services management and health care organization and, in particular, that it can shed light on problems of managing change and, more especially, the relationship between planned and unplanned processes of change. The book grows out of earlier research (Dopson, 1994) on the introduction, following the publication of the Griffiths Report (DHSS, 1983), of general management into the National Health Service (NHS).

Elias is not a sociologist normally associated with health care management; indeed, Eliasian sociology has rarely been used in the study of organizations or management. The details of Eliasian sociology are given in Chapter 3, but a brief overview of its principles is appropriate in this introduction. For Elias, sociology is the study of people. The plural 'people' highlights the critical point that human beings are social beings – they do not exist in a vacuum but are part of networks of social relationships. Elias notes that we are involved in social relationships with people we do not know and of whose existence we may be unaware. This notion contrasts with a very common conception of relationships, namely that relationships are best thought of in terms of face-to-face contacts. A great deal of the empirical work exploring NHS management considers relationships in this latter sense and makes the assumption that people with whom we have personal or direct contact have the greatest impact upon us. Little significant attempt is made in this literature to anchor the actions of managers or management teams in the wider social context of which they are a part.

Elias also stresses that we are affected by the activities of past generations – not only in terms of material things such as buildings, but also in terms of language, educational systems and so on. A key point for Elias is, therefore, that we cannot adequately understand people's actions outside of their social and historical context. Again, many existing studies of NHS management and of management of change within the NHS do not properly locate managers' actions within this broader social and historial context and, because of this, they offer only a partial understanding of management problems and issues.

These complex networks Elias depicts as interdependency ties which necessarily involve power relationships which tend to be unequal across a range of dimensions – for example, in terms of coercive, economic and persuasive power. These networks are always dynamic, that is they are in process. They can be conceived of in more abstract terms as processes such as the division of labour, or nation-state formation, but it is critical to note that these processes only exist in and through the actions of people. These people form complex figurations, hence the term given to Elias's particular approach to the study of people – figurational sociology.

What, then, for those involved in managing change, is the relevance of an understanding of longer-term, unplanned processes? In this context, it is important to remind ourselves that, as Elias (1977, pp. 138–9) has noted, the steady growth of more conscious and deliberate attempts to manage processes of change through the growth of institutionalized forms of social planning is a development which is characteristic of a specific phase of a broader *unplanned* development. Yet those involved in designing and implementing processes of managed social change hardly ever bother to ask questions about the long-term, unplanned structural changes in human societies which have provided the basis, particularly in the twentieth century, for the rapid growth of precisely those kinds of planning projects in which they are themselves involved.

This book uses the implementation of the Griffiths Report as the vehicle for exploring the usefulness of process or figurational sociology in the study of managing change within the NHS. This Report was the product of some nine-months' work, seeking to find out why the NHS continued to consume vast amounts of public resources yet failed, in the government's terms, to be either efficient or effective. The Report was the work of four private-sector managers including the inquiry leader, Roy Griffiths, then managing director and deputy chair of Sainsbury food stores and after whom the Report was named, and was supported by two civil servants. This team was chosen because of its members' business experience. Its task was not to create further major change in the NHS but to make recommendations within the existing system.

Briefly, the Report criticized the NHS on a number of grounds, notably for what was claimed to be its lack of strategic central direction, the absence of individual managerial responsibility, and the lip-service paid to a consumer and performance orientation. It proposed the introduction of general management throughout the NHS. At a national policy level, a supervisory board chaired by the Secretary of State was created to concentrate on the determination of the purpose, objectives and direction of the NHS, deal with resource allocation issues and to monitor the performance of the service. The NHS management board was charged with implementing policies set by the supervisory board and with giving leadership to the NHS. It was to cover all existing NHS management responsibilities, including regional and District Health Authorities (DHAs), Family Practitioner Committees (FPCs), special health authorities and other centrally funded services. Reporting to these two bodies were general managers at regional, district and unit level. It was not assumed that these managers would necessarily have NHS backgrounds and they were seen as critical agents in moving the NHS away from an administrative culture to a general management culture, where accountabilities were clear, decisions would be taken to create a more effective and efficient organization that would meet the needs of its patients (in the Report they are referred to as customers), as well as ensuring good value for money.

The introduction of general managers responsible for local health services meant the end of the previous management arrangements where an administrator, nurse, medical officer and a treasurer along with a representative from hospital medicine and general practice worked together as a consensus team to manage health services. More than previous reorganizations of the NHS in 1974 and 1982, the Griffiths changes were a conscious attempt to move away from a 'boxes and charts' approach to organizational change, to one which sought to disturb organizational processes and ultimately to change the beliefs and values of NHS personnel.

The intention is not to provide a comprehensive summary of the consequences of implementation of the Griffiths report or to offer a general evaluation of the effectiveness of general management. The point is a more simple one, but one that raises an interesting problem in relation to how we can best analyse processes of managed social change. The material presented in the book suggests that the implementation of general management did not work out in the way in which either Sir Roy Griffiths or the government had intended; there were, that is to say, a number of unanticipated consequences of the introduction of general management and, at least in some cases, those consequences were not only unexpected but were actually the very reverse of what had been intended and hoped for by those responsible for initiating these changes. The question which immediately arises, therefore, is how we can account for what a number of studies of general management have identified as a significant gap between the intentions and aspirations expressed in the Griffiths Report, and what the introduction of general management was able to deliver. It is argued that process sociology is helpful in this respect.

THE ORGANIZATION OF THE BOOK

The network of power relationships within the NHS are themselves in process. These relationships are rooted in the history of the NHS and therefore Chapter 2 considers very briefly the issues surrounding the formation of the NHS and its various reorganizations as reported both in the general literature on the NHS and the available ethnographies of local health services management. Details of what has been called figurational or process sociology are given in Chapter 3.

Following a general discussion of the Griffiths Report in Chapter 4, Chapter 5 gives an empirical account of the introduction of general management at district level. The rest of the chapter seeks to explore some of the analyses offered. The concluding chapter reflects on the arguments presented in the book and considers some of the implications for social planning.

2 Reorganizing the NHS: Theory and Practice

INTRODUCTION

Given that the objective of the book is to consider some of the more theoretical issues involved in managed social change, using the example of the introduction of general management in the NHS, it is appropriate to set this example in its proper context. Specifically the chapter documents, firstly, the attempts to reorganize the NHS prior to the introduction of general management and, secondly, what is known about the effects of these attempts. The chapter begins by discussing the emerging concerns about the way in which health services were developing after the formation of the NHS, the build up to the first reorganization in 1974, and the core features of that reorganization. It goes on to explore pressures leading up to the second reorganization in 1982. A central question to be addressed concerns the issue of why the two reorganizations of the NHS, prior to the introduction of general management, took an essentially bureaucratic form. The final section of the chapter focuses on management within such a structure, and briefly reviews the available ethnographies of management of local health services and the more general literature on health service management until 1983.

STRUCTURAL CHANGE AND THE NHS

Examination of historical data documenting the formation of the NHS and the various reorganizations reveals a growing complexity in its organization as well as an increasing interdependence of groups involved in delivering health services. As is well-known, the structure of the NHS in 1948 was a product of bargaining and negotiation carried out in the health policy community. (See Eckstein, 1958 and 1960; Klein, 1983, Chapter 1; and Webster, 1988 for details of the politics involved in the formation of the NHS.) The NHS represented a compromise between those involved in the negotiations (Klein, 1983, p. 26). The government made major concessions to the medical profession – for example, the option of local government control was dismissed, the independent contractor status for GPs was maintained, the principle of private practice and pay beds in NHS hospitals was accepted and consultants were eligible for distinction awards which brought large salary increases. Furthermore, the medical profession exercised a major role in the administration of the services. For their part, the profession lost on the issue of a state-funded and, in effect, salaried service (for GPs this was called 'independent contractor status'). By way of contrast, local authorities lost control of their hospitals as Nye Bevan combined them with the voluntary hospitals within a single system of administration.

By 1970, the NHS had achieved a great deal. In comparison to other industrialized countries, the health indicators such as specific death rates and life expectancy were average, while the costs expressed as a proportion of GNP or national income were much lower than average. Compared to Canada or the USA, the geographical spread of services was good. Prevention of illness services were being developed, and the various public surveys that were carried out tended to show the NHS as a highly-used and much appreciated service. Professional staff were in general supportive of the NHS, although there were demands for increased resources and better pay and working conditions. Indeed, ancillary workers took industrial action during the pay freeze of 1973. (See Draper, Grenholm and Best, 1976, pp. 251–8 for details of the above points, and Bosanquet, 1979 and Seifert, 1992 for a review of industrial relations issues in the NHS at that time.) In general, up until the proposed reorganization in 1974, the views of patients and providers of NHS services – although far from systematically documented – appear to reflect a positive acceptance of the NHS and a feeling that, although efforts should be made to improve it, there should be no question of dismantling or radically altering it.

There were, however, a number of concerns about the way in which health services were developing. A major issue was the growth of the hospital sector *vis-à-vis* general practitioner and community services. For example, capital expenditure in 1970–71 was £114m on hospitals, as compared to £5.1m for loans on health centres and £1.3m for official loans for other general practice buildings (DHSS, 1972). Furthermore, staffing ratios for hospital doctors increased between 1959 and 1969 by 30 per cent, whereas the general practitioner service staffing ratio remained the same as at the commencement of the NHS.

A more general concern was the ability of the NHS to cope with the emerging pressures being placed on it. For example, Draper,

Grenholm and Best argue that by the early 1970s there were four categories of pressures for changing the then existing NHS structure.

1. *Escalating costs and the changing fiscal orientation of the government.* The rise in the proportion of gross national product (GNP) spent on health care was often cited as evidence of this pressure. The UK in 1969 spent 6 per cent of GNP on health compared to 3.5 per cent in 1950 (Rogaly, 1973). Increased costs were related to more advanced medical technology, increased capacity to cure or curtail previously life-threatening diseases, and increased demands for more long-term rehabilitation care.

2. *The changing population structure and patterns of illness.* A decline in the birth rate after the initial postwar boom and the ability to cure more acute conditions as a result of more advanced medical technology meant the population aged (in 1949, the total UK population was 48.9 million and 5.2 million were aged over 65; in 1971, the total UK population was 54 million with 7 million aged over 65). As a consequence of the ageing population, the NHS had to cope with more chronic illness which added to the escalating costs.

3. *Continuing local and regional inequalities.* DHSS figures for the allocation of funds to different parts of the country suggested that the single most important factor in explaining the allocation of funds in this period was the historical legacy of each region. For example in 1950–51, South-Western (London) Metropolitan Hospital Region (the highest spending region) was allocated twice as much money per head of the population as the Sheffield Region (the lowest spending region). By 1971–72 these same regions were still respectively the top and the bottom regions, and the gap had narrowed only slightly (Draper, Grenholm and Best, 1976, p. 263).

4. *Recognition of neglected types of need and an evolving health care philosophy.* During the 1960s a number of scandals, prominent amongst them the Ely Mental Hospital scandal, served to alert the public to the neglect of what were to become known as the Cinderella services; that is, mental health, psycho-geriatrics and community care services as well as the poor links between the hospital and community sectors which threatened 'comprehensive care'. The creation of the Health Advisory Service (HAS) was one response to this neglect. At the same time, there was a significant interest in the benefits to patients of institutional care in relation

to its cost and the benefits afforded to patients from community care (McKeown, 1976; Powles, 1973.) Increasingly, psycho-social skills were seen to be very important if the health professions were to meet the challenges associated with the changing patterns of illness.

Draper, Grenholm and Best argue that in such a dynamic situation as that in which the NHS found itself in the 1970s, one might have expected modifications to the structure of the NHS that fostered the social processes that would enable it to grow and adapt to the changing demands being placed upon it. They argue:

> We would have looked for an organization that would tend to permit genuine devolution of power – for the decentralization of decisions that were not truly national. Equally, with the changes and conflicts over the goals of health care, we would have sought an organization that would foster the process of participation so that all providers and consumers of care could share in the determination of goals.   (Draper, Grenholm and Best, 1976, p. 266)

They go on to argue that 'open' organizational changes would have been a direct and logical response to the pressures discussed earlier. For example, local and regional resource inequalities imply the need for more open discussion of how resource allocation decisions are arrived at; the awareness of the need for greater coordination between policy areas would suggest a looser and less rigid definition of administrative and management roles; an awareness of the need for flexibility to respond to changing policies and priorities would have suggested the need to avoid anything smacking of a 'command hierarchy'. These characteristics would, they argued, facilitate the close monitoring of local needs and priorities and the continuous redefinition of goals – two essential conditions for the successful operation of a system as large, complex and important as the NHS. What emerged as the first reorganization of the NHS was, however, a far cry from an organizational structure built around evolving health needs and patterns of care.

The Conservative Government's proposals that led to the 1974 reorganization of the NHS emphasized the importance of improving its management efficiency. No clear elaboration was given as to what was meant by effective management. However, the clearest indication of what was meant was contained in the consultative document announcement that two 'expert studies' had been commissioned by the DHSS: Brunel University's health service organization research unit had been commissioned to consider detailed management arrangements for the new authorities and their staff, looking in particular at role relationships and the management consultants, and McKinsey and Co. Inc. had been engaged to conduct trials with a few Hospital Management Committees (HMCs) (Levitt and Wall, 1989, p. 14).

The final report on the management arrangements for the reorganized NHS, known as the Grey Book, did not appear until the end of 1972. The DHSS issued a number of circulars to health authorities. These circulars and a newsheet – *NHS Reorganization News* – were the only information available as there was very little public debate on the reorganization (Levitt and Wall, 1989, p. 15). The NHS Reorganization Act was given Royal Assent on 5 July 1973, and the final structure is shown below in Figure 2.1.

The new arrangements for the NHS abolished the former tripartite administrative structure and established a structure with only parts of the environmental health services remaining under local authority control. The Area Health Authorities (AHAs) were corporately responsible for health care in geographical areas which were, on the whole, coterminous with the local authority metropolitan districts and non-metropolitan counties, except in the case of London AHAs where there were groupings of boroughs. In a single district AHA there was an Area Team of Officers (ATO) which supported the AHA members and held delegated executive power. Under the original 1974 arrangements, each AHA had 15 members, and the new Labour Government announced minor changes to the reorganization in the consultative paper *Democracy in the NHS* (DHSS, 1974). These changes included an increase in the local authority membership of both AHAs and Regional Health Authorities (RHAs) to one-third of the total, and the inclusion of two additional NHS staff members on each authority. The AHAs were responsible to RHAs for the running of services. In areas which had teaching hospitals within their boundaries, the health authorities were responsible for their administration and were known as AHA/Ts. In all there were 90 English AHAs, 16 of them in Greater London.

The AHAs were grouped together under 14 RHAs whose role was to translate national policies into a framework of regional objectives. RHAs were also charged with allocating capital revenue resources to ensure that national objectives were met, as well as feeding back to the

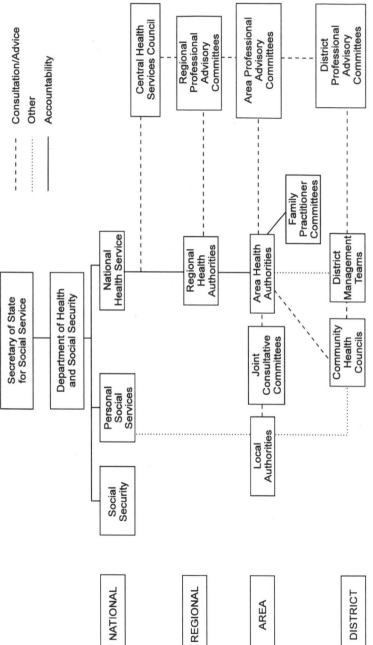

Figure 2.1 Management arrangements for the reorganized National Health Service

Source: DHSS, 1972.

Department of Health and Social Security (DHSS) data about achievement of objectives and potential developments. The RHA's role was greatly influenced by the introduction of a national system of planning for health services in 1976, which was to be comprehensive in its coverage, encompassing all resources (physical and human) and all services. The system was to involve not only planners but also professional staff through advisory committees, health care planning teams and the public, via Community Health Councils (CHCs). Central to the planning system were the twin concepts of guidelines and plans. Government guidelines informed regional plans and plans then informed guidelines. It was hoped that the planning system would be the vehicle to achieve the shift in the balance of care from the acute sector to community care which had become a government policy with the publication of *Priorities for Health and Personal Social Services in England* (DHSS, 1976). There were no direct equivalents to regions in Scotland, Wales or Northern Ireland, where the equivalent to the English region was a common service agency.

The districts were intended to be the smallest units where the full range of general health and social services could be provided. Districts were to have populations of around 250 000 people. The key features of the NHS organization at district level are shown in Figure 2.2 and include District Management Teams (DMTs), District Medical Committees (DMCs), Health Care Planning Teams (HCPTs) and Community Health Councils (CHCs).

Each DMT comprised a nursing officer, a finance officer, an administrator and a specialist in community medicine. It also included two members of the District Medical Committee (DMC), usually the chair and vice-chair, who represented local hospital consultants and general practitioners and who were the only members of the management team to receive special payment because their responsibilities involved work outside their normal duties. These district officers were charged with managing and coordinating many of the operational aspects of NHS services within their localities and helping formulate the policies and plans for the future.

A common feature of all teams in all parts of Britain was to be their mode of decision-making: they were to be '. . . consensus bodies, that is, decisions . . . need the agreement of each of the team members' (DHSS, 1972, p. 15). In the event of a difference of opinion between team members, the health authority was to be called in to resolve the issue concerned. Harrison (1982) notes that although the formal proposition for introducing consensus management was set out by a

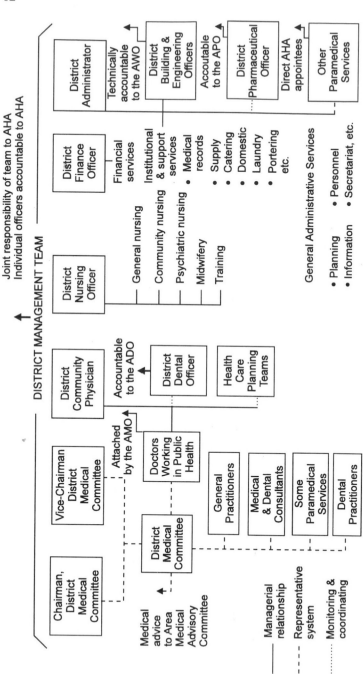

Figure 2.2 Framework of the district organisation

Source: *Management Arrangements for the Reorganization of the NHS:* DHSS, 1972.

study group of DHSS and NHS officers assisted by Messrs McKinsey and Co. and the health services organization research unit of Brunel University, it is possible to see consensus decision-making as 'an extension and formalization of a *de facto* practice which had been gaining ground in the NHS over a number of years'. He notes competing rationales for the introduction of consensus management which he describes as unitary and pluralistic (Harrison, 1982, p. 378). The unitary rationale is based on the premise that the parties involved in the decision-making process each have objectives which do not fundamentally conflict. The emphasis is thus upon joint problem-solving to solve management problems, which bears a marked resemblance to rational prescriptive models of decision-making (Hunter, 1979, p. 323). The pluralistic rationale allows for the existence of legitimately differing interests within the organization. It is a pragmatic recognition that the NHS is organized around functional and professional hierarchies and collegially organized professions, and that no practical alternative to team management exists, as a mode of decision-making by such teams (Harrison, 1982, p. 379). Interestingly, team management sat within a bureaucratic structure which meant that decisions from the team had to receive approval not only from the health authority but also from the management tier above.

Other bodies associated with the 1974 reorganization are briefly described below. The DMC consisted of ten members drawn from hospital and community medical staff (including dentists). The HCPTs were set up to draw together professionals concerned with particular groups of clients or patients. Each team was to examine the existing level of service and make recommendations to the DMT for improvements. Membership of the teams was decided by the DMT and formally approved by the AHA. Later HCPTs changed their title to District Planning Teams (DPT), but their function remained the same.

The CHCs were, in theory, to act as public watchdogs with regard to the development of health services (and hospital closures). They were not part of the formal management structure but were allowed access to NHS plans and premises. They were to meet with the AHA annually and publish reports to which the AHAs were obliged to reply. Most CHCs had between 18 and 30 members of whom half were appointed by the local authority, one-third by local voluntary organizations and the remainder selected by RHA. CHC membership was worked out principally on the basis of the resident district population. Generally each CHC had two full-time staff – the secretary and his or her assistant. Research on CHCs suggest they were relatively weak in terms of influencing the policy processes (Brown, 1975, p. 193; Ham, 1977).

The 1974 reorganization was intended by government to meet four goals:

1. To unify health services by bringing under one authority all the services previously administered by the Regional Hospital Boards (RHBs), HMCs, boards of governors, executive councils and local health authorities.
2. To improve coordination between health authorities and related government services, in order to achieve a more integrated service.
3. To improve the management of the NHS. To this end the 'Grey Book' set out very detailed notes on the functions of each tier as well as providing job descriptions for health authority officers. Other examples given by the government of better management included the introduction of consensus management and the principle of maximum delegation downwards, matched by accountability upwards embedded in the new planning system.
4. To provide effective central control of the money spent on the NHS, thus ensuring value for money.

It is interesting to compare these goals with the major pressures for change identified by Draper, Grenholm and Best earlier in this chapter. What is missing from official documents is any commentary on how the reorganization would assist the consumers of health care – that is patients – or the communities which local health services served. Additionally, it is difficult to imagine how the essentially mechanistic command and control structure characteristic of the reorganization could begin to deal with the complex pressures on the provision of health care or influence the then existing patterns of health care delivery discussed earlier. Furthermore, Draper, Grenholm and Best argued that the 1974 reorganization constituted a shift away from the principles of participative democracy on which the NHS was founded, and towards an authoritarian bureaucracy to which they attribute the following characteristics:

Authoritarian bureaucracies aspire to work from the top down; decisions are made at the top of the bureaucracy and, in the bureaucratic idea, move progressively down to the working level. People at that level are not expected to make the decisions that determine their work nor the conditions under which the work is carried out. When people at working level are the recipients of services, as in the NHS, they are even less expected to contribute to the processes of deciding what those services should be. The primary obligation of both providers and recipients is to know their place, and to follow the orders of their betters, that is, the providers, in the case of the patients, and hierarchical superiors in the case of the providers.

(Draper, Grenholm and Best, 1976, p. 286)

In their view, the 1974 reorganization was an important indicator that society was moving away from the idea of democracy as participative and toward the idea that democracy is administered.

It is difficult to see how the structure which emerged could be said to have met the specific goals of the reorganization. It is true that the reorganization went some way to producing an integrated service. For example, the new AHA boundaries were coterminous with local authority boundaries (that is, they had identical boundaries), underlying the need for close collaboration between all parts of the health service. However, there were significant anomalies. For instance, FPCs continued to have direct links with the DHSS, and continued to administer contracts of GPs, dentists, opticians and pharmacists. In addition, not all local government health services were transferred to the NHS with, most notably, environmental health services remaining within local government. These anomalies threatened the goal of improved coordination as indeed did the indifference of the government to the psychological or social effects on health of general social and economic policies, such as those related to taxation, housing or transport and the importance of closer links with social services (Draper, Grenholm and Best, 1976, p. 276).

The 'special contribution' of Keith Joseph (the then Minister of Health), that is the emphasis placed on improving the management of the NHS, drew a great deal of fire from the health service press at the time. Specifically it was criticized for reflecting an essentially outdated concept of management based on the importance of hierarchy and control. In part, this criticism was based on and reflects the progressive delineation of skill areas that had taken place in parallel with the moves towards reorganization (see the Salmon Report, 1966, which made recommendations for the development of a senior nursing staff structure and the Cogwheel Report, 1967, which advocated special groupings that could arrange administrative medical work more efficiently).

The emphasis on hierarchy and control is evident if one looks at the limited opportunities for public participation in decision-making. As a result of the reorganization, power was largely concentrated at the upper levels of the new structure. Members of RHAs, the regional chair and the AHA chair were chosen by government. AHA members had to be approved by the RHA. Members of the new authorities were chosen on the basis of personal qualities rather than as representatives. In these respects, policy-control is clearly seen as the province of managers and the Centre rather than of those directly affected by the policies; thus the patients' voice was channelled through the CHC, a body with no executive power and which subsequently had little impact on policy decisions (Brown, 1975; Klein and Lewis, 1976; Ham, 1980; Haywood and Alaszewski, 1980). Johnson, writing about CHCs, notes three key issues facing them: deciding who is the community and what the community wants; influencing health care policy when CHCs have 'no teeth'; and dealing with the power relationships which separate the professional from the consumer (Johnson, 1976, p. 91). The reorganization documents gave no indication of how CHCs were to find out what the public wanted or how to influence decisions taken higher up.

Another example of a shift from participative democracy towards authoritarian bureaucracy can be found in changes to the role of the Medical Officer of Health (MOH). This job traditionally was a professional role, with the MOH being given the brief to speak out in the public interest. Under the new arrangements, the MOH became a community physician tied into the management structure whose task it was to assess the needs of the population by technical means.

Draper, Grenholm and Best warn that it would be inaccurate to characterize all the features of the reorganization as being those of a techno-bureaucracy; some features, such as the principle of 'clinical autonomy' for doctors continued the pattern of professional organization.[1] Consensus management also reveals a different approach, which sits uncomfortably alongside notions of hierarchy and control.

It is important to examine the broader social context at the time of the reorganization in order to begin to understand why the reorganization took the form it did. In the late 1960s and early 1970s, scientific management principles were in vogue (see Taylor, 1947, and Fayol, 1949, for clearest examples of this). Effective management, according to this tradition, was contingent on management defining the right needs and priorities for the organization as well as emphasizing the importance of organizing, commanding, coordinating and controlling.

The assumption was that organizational problems were due to the failure of the rationality of the organization and could be corrected by an array of management techniques. This tradition was mirrored in health services research at the time which consisted mainly of evaluating biological results of health services often via random control trials. There was little research done exploring how the public perceived the organizational and managerial issues of the NHS and little research of managerial processes in the NHS.

The reorganization was also indicative of the enthusiasm for structural reform prevalent in the 1960s and early 1970s, associated with the view that technology is a morally and politically neutral medium of social progress (Alaszewski, Tether and McDonnell, 1981, p. 5). The common characteristics of structural change in the public sector in this period included: an emphasis on service coordination or integration, an emphasis on community involvement, attempts to incorporate professionals in management and a concern with skilled and efficient management. The similarities in the changes in public sector services can be partly explained by restructurings in the public sector being overseen by a common stock – the Brunel health service organization research unit and the consultants, McKinsey and Co.

The poor quality of the press and media coverage of the reorganization meant that some of the obvious anomalies inherent in the restructuring and the wider issues raised so cogently by Draper, Grenholm and Best, were not aired. The first BBC TV programme on the reorganization was broadcast on 6 July 1973 after the Bill had received Royal Assent (Draper, Grenholm and Best, 1976). The public were, in the main, oblivious to the changes. Eskin, in her survey of public knowledge of the reorganization, found that only 10 out of her 100 sample knew the reorganization had occurred (Eskin and Newton, 1977).

Just as the incoming Labour Government in 1974 had inherited a reorganization not of its own making, the new Conservative Government elected in May 1979 had to respond to a Royal Commission not of its own creation. The government issued a consultative document on the structure and management of the NHS in England and Wales, *Patients First*, in December 1979 (DHSS, 1979), which adopted a rather different line from the 1974 restructuring. It argued there should be more delegation so that decisions were made nearer patients, that DHAs should be strengthened and the area tier removed. In addition it argued for the simplification of the professional consultative machinery.

Patients First had a four-month deadline for consultation. The government's proposals were published in July 1980 in a Circular (DHSS, 1980), and there was little change from the proposals outlined in *Patients First*. The circular set out the criteria for the establishment of DHAs as follows:

> DHAs should be established for the smallest geographical areas within which it is possible to carry out the integrated planning, provision and development of primary care and other community health services, together with those services normally associated with the District General Hospital (DGH), including those for the elderly, mentally ill and mentally handicapped. The new authorities should not necessarily be self-sufficient in all these services. They should as far as possible comprise natural communities and the boundaries of one or more DHAs should normally be coterminus with the boundary of the social services or education authorities.
> (Chaplin, 1982, p. 11)

To minimize disruption, the new DHAs were to follow the boundaries of existing districts or single-district areas. RHAs were required to draw up proposals for dividing their regions into districts and, after consulting local interests, submit them to the DHSS. The new DHAs were formally to take over responsibility from AHAs on 1 April 1982. RHAs were unaffected by the dissolution of the AHAs and creation of the DHAs, except that a few boundary changes were made in the Thames regions where new districts were created which crossed existing regional boundaries.

In the new DHAs the management teams remained the same, involving an administrator, treasurer, medical officer, nursing officer, consultant and general practitioner representative who were accountable to DHA members. The circular emphasized that consensus management must not be allowed to blur the individual responsibility of team officers for the services that they manage, and that the administrator was to have an important coordinating role. The new district authorities were to arrange their services into units of management (often centred on a hospital or a community unit). These were not closely defined, but the DHA was to decide what was desirable and possible within the cost limits allowed.

Instead of 90 AHAs, there were to be 190 DHAs. FPCs continued to act independently from DHAs as they had done in relation to AHAs. CHCs were to be retained, one for each district. The number of mem-

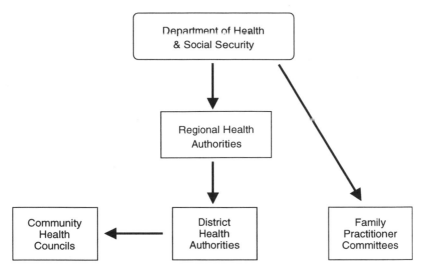

Figure 2.3   The structure of the NHS after 1982

Source: Levitt and Wall, 1989.

bers of the health authorities at region and district was to be reduced. The structure of the NHS after 1982 is shown above in Figure 2.3.

In the second reorganization documents there was less emphasis on the ideology of rational and scientific management. Alaszewski, Tether and McDonnell (1981, p. 13) highlight five areas of difference from the 1974 proposals:

- a greater emphasis on patients;
- a search for a natural community for administrative units;
- increased local autonomy;
- simplified managerial relationships, and
- a simplified process of decision legitimation.

They claim:

> Whereas the 1974 reorganization was about organization and efficiency, the new [restructuring] is about patients; 1974 involved centralization, the new emphasis is local autonomy, 1974 was about refined and sophisticated managerial relations, the new [restructuring]...will create simple and robust relations.
>
> (Alaszweski, Tether and McDonnell, 1981, p. 3).

Nonetheless both reorganizations were essentially bureaucratic attempts to manage the complex and evolving demands on health services and meant that the complex interdependencies of groups and individuals working within the NHS became more complex.

WHY A BUREAUCRATIC REORGANIZATION?

The level of debate concerning why the NHS took the essentially bureaucratic form it had up to 1983 is, frankly, disappointing. There are some excellent histories of the formation of the NHS (Willcocks, 1967; Foot, 1973; and Webster, 1988), some informative textbooks (Levitt and Wall, 1989 being a particularly useful one), but little analysis of the social-structural processes that have played a part in the various reforms of the NHS. In his book *The Politics of the NHS*, Klein argues that the NHS emerged in 1948 as an extremely complex structure because policy-makers tried to achieve a variety of policy aims, while seeking to preserve consensus and avoid conflict. The conflicting policy aims he spelled out were: 'to promote managerial efficiency, to satisfy the medical profession, to create an effective hierarchy for transmitting national policy, but also to give scope to managers at the periphery' (Klein, 1983, p. 99). However, most of the debate about the reorganizations of the NHS has centred on the view that change is difficult because of the 'special' characteristics of the NHS and the complex issues involved in health care delivery as reviewed by Draper, Grenholm and Best. A brief discussion of the 'special' characteristics of the NHS is given below, as well as an indication of why these characteristics render a bureaucratic response inappropriate.

Those writing in the public administration tradition highlight the following factors as increasing the difficulties of successfully introducing change within the Health Service: less market exposure resulting in less incentive to reduce cost or to operate efficiently; a wider stakeholder interest than the private sector, most notably involving politicians, taxpayers and voters; the existence of pressure group influences because resources are both finite and limited and are distributed as an act of political will; and the existence of customers, clients, consumers and citizens which makes it difficult to define who the customer is. Flynn *et al.* (1988) argue that keeping abreast of changes in the 'environment' is more difficult for public sector managers because of the perennial uncertainty as to which specific issue will in practice become politically significant.

Organizational constraints are often cited as yet more 'special characteristics' of the public sector that make introducing change difficult. Smith, Ring and Perry (1985) put forward five key constraints on public managers at the organizational level:

- policy directives tend to be more ill-defined for public than for private organizations;
- the relative openness of decision-making creates greater constraints;
- public sector policy makers are generally subject to more direct and sustained influence from interest groups;
- public sector management must cope with time constraints that are more artificial than those that confront private sector management; and
- policy legitimisation coalitions are less stable in the public sector and are more prone to disintegrate during policy implementation.

Another organizational factor often cited in this literature as impeding the implementation of change is the existence of established professional structures. A point often made is that since the NHS is a highly professionalized organization, relying on high-trust collaborative work relationships, the two major modes of controlling behaviour – professional and bureaucratic authority – fundamentally conflict, hence jeopardizing change. Talcott Parsons has been credited with prising open the notions of profession and bureaucracy. In a much-quoted footnote inserted by Parsons into his translation of Weber's work (Weber, 1964), Parsons argues that the authority of expertise constitutes a special problem for the bureaucratic organization (Davies, 1983, p. 182). Scott (1966) offers perhaps the clearest statement of the popular conception of the two institutional forms. A professional, he notes, carries out a complete task; he or she does so on the basis of special knowledge acquired through training; he or she is loyal to the community of equal professionals rather than to the bureaucratic organization; as a practitioner he or she has arrived at a terminal status and seeks no higher position within the organization. This contrasts with the caricature of the bureaucrat who is seen to carry out a limited set of tasks which must be coordinated with others; the training involved in becoming a bureaucrat is relatively short and accomplished within the organization; supervision of work is done by a hierarchical superior and the bureaucrat is subject to sanctions if he or she does not follow the rules. Generally loyalty and career are tied

Table 2.1   A model of professional–bureaucratic conflict

	Bureaucracy	Professionalism
Task	Partial, interdependent with others	Complete, sole work
Training	Short, within the organization, a specialized skill	Long, outside the organization a total skill
Legitimation for act	Is following rules	Is doing what is to the best of his knowledge correct
Compliance	Is supervised	Is socialized
Loyalty	To the organization	To the profession
Career	Ascent in the organizational hierarchy	Often no further career steps in the organization

Source: Davies, 1983.

to the organization (Davies, 1983, p. 178).[2] Table 2.1 above, devised by Celia Davies (1983) and drawing on Scott's work, sums up these divergent perspectives.

Studies of relationships within hospitals have questioned the view that health care organizations consist of a rigidly structured set of relationships (Szasz and Hollender, 1956; Strauss, 1978; Bloor and Horobin, 1974; Jeffrey and Sachs, 1983). Although such studies can be criticized for ignoring wider structural constraints on behaviour, they are useful in pointing out the lack of a traditional bureaucratic hierarchy within certain aspects of hospital and general practice work. Strauss and his colleagues introduced the concept of 'negotiated order' to elucidate hospital life (Strauss *et al.* 1983). Their analysis is based on the assumption that within hospitals, official rules are rarely specific enough to guide people's daily or hourly interactions, which are therefore subject to negotiation (Morgan, Calnan and Manning, 1985, p. 150). Strauss *et al.* suggest that daily life in health care settings is organized around a series of bargains struck and forgotten, or renegotiated from time to time.

Another source of support for the view that the NHS is not suited to a bureaucratic structure can be found in the organizational behaviour literature concerning organizational structure in the private sector. The trend since the early 1980s has been to move away from pyramidal bureaucratic structures to more flexible organizational arrangements, a more participative management style and an increased emphasis on teamwork. The catalyst for these trends has been a recognition of the increasing complexity organizations have to face, for example increased competition, political pressures for change, information technology and social pressures for change such as the movement towards equal opportunities. The argument has been that flexible organizational structures are best-suited to cope with this more turbulent environment (Peters and Waterman, 1982; Handy, 1989). Health service organizational theorists as well as medical sociologists have shown a great reluctance to consider recent trends in the private sector in making their case for a change in the structure and organization of the NHS.

Finally, it has been argued that a bureaucratically structured NHS will not assist in meeting the health needs of the population served. Various authors writing in the medical sociology literature note that bureaucracy is slow in reacting to changes in health needs (Doyal, 1980; LeGrand, 1980; Townsend and Davidson, 1982) and is not sensitive to the ways in which health needs are filtered. Various studies have demonstrated that health services deal only with a small proportion of health problems present in a population at any particular time, for most symptoms occur without any contact with formal health services. The findings of Wadsworth *et al.* (1971) reported in Table 2.2, are typical of retrospective studies in this area.

Table 2.2 shows that 95 per cent of a sample of 1000 adults had experienced symptoms in the 14 days prior to interview. Only one in five people had consulted a doctor, and class, gender and age appear to be significant influences on whether a doctor is consulted (Dingwall, 1976; Cartwright and Anderson, 1981; Pill and Stott, 1982). Such studies confirm the existence of a significant clinical iceberg: that is, health services treat only the tip of the total of ill-health.

We know from the medical sociology literature that health care problems pass through a series of filters. The initial filter is the

Table 2.2   Two-week incidence of symptoms and subsequent behaviour in a random sample of 1000 adults living in London

Individuals with no symptoms	49
Individuals with symptoms taking no action	188
Individuals with symptoms taking non-medical action	562
General practitioner patients	168
Hospital out-patients	28
Hospital in-patients	5
Total	1000

Source: Adapted from Wadsworth *et al.*, 1971.

person-with-the-illness who makes the judgement, perhaps after consulting family or friends, about presenting himself or herself to a
health practitioner. A second filter is the GP, who is a filter in two
ways: firstly there is research evidence that GPs may not
recognize many problems presented to them, and secondly the GP's
decision to refer is a significant filter. The third filter is the hospital
consultant: once a patient reaches the hospital, it is the consultant
who decides whether and how to treat the patient, what tests to
request, when to admit and when to discharge. A bureaucratic system
does not cope with these processes well for two main reasons. Firstly,
as a formal centralized system it can only cope with conventional
methods of entry and it relies on the GP to trigger-off processes to
deal with people's demands for health care. Secondly, the lack of
community participation in decisions relating to health care provision
and the absence of communication channels with the community
means that a bureaucratic system is insensitive to many of the
population's health care needs and preferences for the delivery of
health care.

There are, however, various aspects of providing health care that
are effectively managed by bureaucratic procedures. For example,
collecting data on demographic change and anticipating the effects
of such change on demand for health services; and monitoring tech-
nological change and advances in scientific medicine and examining
the consequences of scientific advances in terms of shifts in disease
prevalence and their impact on the most suitable type of care (that is,
acute or community).

Bureaucratic procedures may also be useful in overseeing the allocation of resources, both to the NHS and within it. Until 1983,
bureaucratic procedures were used in the NHS to redistribute
resources to promote geographical equity and to alter the priorities
between services. To achieve the former, the Department of Health
used methods recommended by the Resource Allocation Working
Party (RAWP) in making allocations to regions, and regions made
district allocations on a similar basis (although each region varied
somewhat in its method for sub-regional allocations). The RAWP
method of allocation was based on capitation (the number of people
served by an authority or board) and not on the services actually
provided. But because residents of one area often use the services of
another, RAWP allocations also tried to take account of these cross-
boundary flows. The adequacy of the capitation element and the
adjustment for cross-boundary flows were contentious.

The second form of redistribution of resources – altering the priorities between services – similarly drew on bureaucratic processes. For example, the 1962 NHS hospital plan introduced a programme for the building of new acute hospitals, and when these hospitals were completed there was generous funding of their revenue consequences. Then, in the 1970s, new priorities emerged, in particular the need to improve services which had been neglected, notably services for the mentally ill and handicapped, the elderly and children. The emphasis has been on shifting the balance of care away from institutions to the community, supported by statutory or voluntary services. This saw an increase in the number of agencies involved, creating enormous problems of coordination of care and in devising suitable budgetary and financial frameworks to ensure good services.

Bureaucratic procedures may also help to ensure that the need to measure outcomes of health care are put firmly on the agenda of those working in the delivery of health services. However, up until 1983 remarkably little effort had gone into assessing outcomes in a systematic fashion or to examining ways of assessing client-satisfaction.

The government in 1974, and again in 1982, chose to seek bureaucratic solutions to important value judgements such as 'what is health' and 'what should health services do' (Alaszewski, Tether and McDonnell, 1981, p. 12) and ignored the complex and evolving demands facing health care services and the ways in which it might be possible to meet these in the context of financial constraints. This is in part an understandable response, given the complexity of such judgements and the difficulties of implementing change in a context as complex as the NHS.

EMPIRICAL STUDIES OF THE NHS MANAGEMENT

A useful source of data to explore further the difficulties of introducing change in the NHS is the various empirical studies of local health services. This work consistently questions the assumptions of both the 1974 and 1982 restructuring to the effect that management is a rational process and that policy is made by the Centre, transmitted to the periphery and implemented there. Those working in local health care systems can, and do, circumvent national policy effectively.

Stephen Harrison has provided a summary of health service management research between 1948 and 1983 documented in Table 2.3 (Harrison, 1988).

Table 2.3 Empirical research in the NHS, 1948–83

Author(s) and publication date	Fieldwork	Scale and scope	Methods and sources
Forsyth (1966)	1964	One RHB & its HMCs	Questionnaire, documents
Rowbottom et al. (1973)	1966–72	One RHB & 9 HMCs	Interviews, action research
Committee of Enquiry into Ely Hospital (1969)	1967–68	One hospital	Formal inquiry
Brown (1979) Brown et al. (1975)	1972–75	One Area Health Authority and its predecessors	Interviews, questionnaires, documents, observation
Haywood (1977)	1974–75	205 CHCs	Questionnaire
Klein and Lewis (1976)	1975–77	12 Scottish Health Boards	Questionnaire, interviews, documents, observation in 2 Boards
Hunter (1979, 1980, 1984)	1975–77 (re 1948/74)	One RHB	Documents, interviews
Ham (1981)	1975–76	17 CHCs, 60 CHC secretaries	Action research
Hallas (1976)	1975–78	DHSS, 2 RHAS 4 AHAs and associated teams	Documents, interviews, observation
Haywood et al. (1979) Haywood (1979) Elcock and Haywood (1980) Haywood and Alaszewski (1980)	1976–79	2 Area Health Authorities	Documents, interviews, observation
Barnard et al. (1979, 1980) Lee and Mills (1982)	1976–78	SHHD, Planning Council, One Scottish Health Board	Documents, interviews, observation
Wiseman (1979)	1977	DHSS, Welsh Office, SHHD, 3 RHAs, 6 Area Authorities 8 Districts, 6 CHCs (in England, Wales, Scotland & N Ireland)	Interviews
Kogan et al. (1978)			

Study	Year	Subject	Formal inquiry
Committee of Inquiry into Normansfield Hospital (1978)	1978	One hospital	Interviews, questionnaires, documents
Harrison (1981) Barnard and Harrison (1986)	1978–82	Health Authorities in England	Interviews, observations
Stewart et al. (1980)	1979	32 District Administrators, 9 Area Administrators	
Harrison (1981b)	1979–80	DHSS, professional associates	Interviews, documents
Hardy (1986)	1979–80	2 Hospital closures	Interviews, documents
Stocking (1985)	1980–83	22 innovations in general: 4 detailed cases in RHAs and 12 districts	Interviews, documents, questionnaires
Rathwell (1987)	1980–84	One HA	Interviews, documents
Glennerster et al. (1983)	1980–81	2 DHAs, 2 Local Authorities, London	Interviews
Schulz and Harrison (1983)	1981	19 Management Teams	Interviews, documents, some observation
Ham (1986)	1981–85	2 DHAS	Action research
Harrison et al. (1984a)	1982	72 managers	Interviews, documents
Thompson (1986)	1982–84	7 Management teams	Interviews, documents
Haywood (1983) Haywood and Ranade (1985)	1982–84	6 DHAs (members)	Documents, interviews, observation, repertory grid
Forte (1986)	1983–84	1 District	Documents, interviews

Source: Harrison (1988) *Shifting the Frontier* (pp. 32–5).

There are several interesting features of this table:

1. There are relatively few studies.
2. There is a relative increase in the number of studies following the 1974 reorganization.
3. Very little empirical work has been done on professional management arrangements or management at the DHSS level.
4. Studies have focused on the general management of health services rather than on the role of professionals, specifically clinicians, in management.
5. This body of research, small as it is, has not informed the various NHS policy documents.

A review of the existing ethnographies of local health services indicates a number of areas of consensus and, interestingly, the findings of studies conducted before 1974 are remarkably similar to those of later studies. Stephen Harrison provides a neat set of propositions which summarize common research findings:

1. Managers were not the most influential actors in the health service.
2. Managerial behaviour was problem-driven rather than objective-driven.
3. Managers were reluctant to question the value of existing patterns of service or to propose major changes in them.
4. Managers behaved as if other groups of employees, rather than the public, were the clients of the health service (Harrison, 1990, p. 31).

Proposition 1   Managers were not the most influential actors in the health service

This proposition is in one sense not surprising since, if one looks at the formal accountability structure before 1983, managers – that is member of the consensus management teams – are accountable to the local health authority, led by the chair. This would lead one to believe that members of the authority should be the most influential people in the management of local health services. However, research into the role of health authorities and, indeed, the role of the chair, reveals that health authorities are relatively impotent in terms of influencing local health care policy, and chairs often lack influence over either the health authority or the management team.

This general view is confirmed by many of the available ethnographies. Brown notes that decisions about the shape of the service, in his case study area of Humberside, were made technocratically, with the minimum of involvement by lay authority members (Brown, 1979, p. 122). Ham in his longitudinal study of the role of members in two health authorities describes members as marginal participants in the policy process (Ham, 1981, p. 127), as do Haywood and Alaszweski (1980, pp. 84–109).

Studies have put forward a number of explanations as to why health authority members are ineffective: there are no real choices to be made locally and therefore no issues to facilitate a distinctive contribution from members; inappropriate selection; lack of preparation and poor training of members; poor information given to members and increased control by the Centre which has served to erode health authority influence (Haywood and Alaszweski, 1980; Haywood 1983; Haywood and Ranade, 1985; Ham, 1986).

Several studies note that the key to understanding how decisions are made and resources allocated in health authorities is the power of the medical profession. Drawing on Alford's work (1975), Ham suggests that in Leeds RHB:

The history of hospital planning between 1948 and 1974 can be seen as the history of corporate rationalizers represented by regional board planners, trying to challenge the established interests of the medical profession, with the community hardly in earshot.

(Ham, 1981, p. 75)

A number of studies echo Ham's point. A statistically-based analysis of the influence of the medical profession on strategic issues was carried out by Haywood and Alaszweski (see Figure 2.4 below). They consider the use of an increment of 28 per cent for NHS spending (the Office of Health Economics calculation) between 1970 and 1977 in order to see what that indicates about the extent of managerial control. For this reason they concentrate on the hospital services. Haywood and Alaszweski point out the following major findings from Figure 2.4:

1. The increase in the numbers of hospital staff has not been matched by an equivalent increase in the number of patients.
2. Whilst some of the growth in personnel (which continued in 1977–78) was pre-empted by national decisions (for example shorter

30

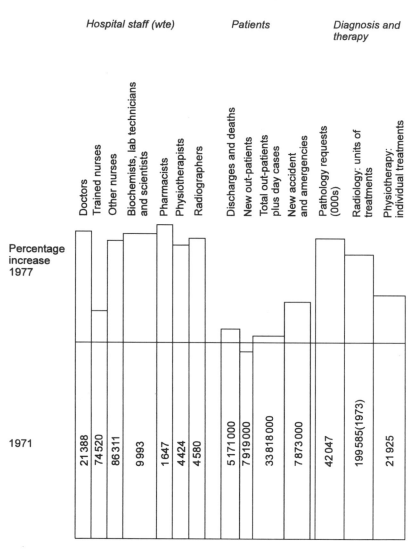

Figure 2.4 A statistically-based analysis of the influence of the medical
profession on strategic issues, 1971–77

Note: These figures refer to 1973–7 because of a significant change in units
of measurement in 1973.
Sources: DHSS, *Health and Personal Social Services Statistics for England*
(HMSO, London); Department summaries of offical returns to the DHSS.
Not all figures are directly comparable because of changes in definitions.
Broad trends are, however, unaffected.

hours, longer holidays), the size of the increment suggests some leeway for a local say in its distribution.

3. The small rise in inpatients treated (though there were far more day-patients) and the static number of outpatients (though there was a sizeable increase in the number of accidents and emergencies), reflects decisions not to use these additional resources to increase throughput.

4. Diagnostic and therapy departments were the principal beneficiaries of additional resources made available to health authorities, and the number of scientists, technicians, physiotherapists and radiographers increased significantly.

5. The major use of the increment was in diagnosis, testing and therapy, with a fairly static number of patients rather than the admission of more of them into the hospital system.

Haywood and Alaszweski conclude from their scrutiny of the data that the crucial element in local decisions on the way the increments should be spent has been the development of clinical practice, and that management has responded to these developments rather than controlled or directed them (Haywood and Alaszweski, 1980, p. 106).

Stocking's study of four innovations (regional secure units, changing patients' waking times, rickets among Asians and day-case surgery) are fascinating examples of how need and solution as seen by those working at the Centre may not fit in with attitudes and opportunities of those at the periphery. Each case study indicates how often the need to manage a service effectively has been tempered by attitudes about clinical freedom and demonstrates the complexity of decision-making in the NHS because of the presence of many powerful, and not always compatible, individuals and interests (Stocking, 1985).

The influence of the medical profession on national arrangements for health care management is well documented (Eckstein, 1958; Forsyth, 1966; Haywood and Alaszweski, 1980). However, ethnographies of local health care systems note a marked contrast between doctors' performance on a national and local stage. Nationally, doctors have taken a lead in securing a position of influence in both the formation of the NHS and subsequent reorganization. However, on the local stage, there appears to be a great reluctance on the part of doctors to get involved in local management of health services. Representatives of the profession are shown to be reluctant to give the time to the demands of a representative role (Brown, 1979, p. 140) and feel vulnerable when taking decisions because of a lack of information and for fear of offending their constituency (Schultz and Harrison, 1983, p. 29). In part, the reluctance to get involved in management can be explained by the overcomplicated professional advisory machinery created in 1974, but also because doctors have a great influence on the service without necessarily being in formally defined administrative roles.

The power of hospital clinicians to shape health services has been attributed to many factors including: the concessions made to the doctors in 1948 (Willcocks, 1967; Eckstein, 1958 and 1960); the spread of the epidemic iatrogenesis which has cost people their liberty with regard to their own bodies (Illich, 1975); the role of doctors as the agents of capitalism, benefitting from a capitalist system (Navarro, 1976; and the objectification of the body (Foucault, 1973). The origin of medical power can, however, be traced back much further. Waddington (1984) notes the importance of the 1858 Medical Act and of the formalization of codes of medical ethics in facilitating the development of a single, relatively unified profession, thus enhancing the power of all medical practitioners.

A number of studies suggest that RHAs, CHCs, local authorities and trade unions have little influence over local health policy except with respect to specific matters. Furthermore, these studies suggest that second to the doctors in terms of influence over local health care policy are the administrators, primarily because of their access to information (Stewart, Smith, Blake and Wingate, 1980, pp. 81–3; Haywood and Alaszewski, 1980; Ham, 1981).

Proposition 2   Managerial behaviour was problem-driven rather than objective-driven in character

In Stewart's study of a group of district administrators (DAs), only a few administrators dealt with strategic issues and most concerned themselves with *ad hoc* referred issues. Stewart uses Belbin's model of groups (Belbin, 1991) to discuss the types of roles adopted by the DA. She notes that the 'shaper' role, characterized by initiation and influence towards objectives, was a role that few DAs adopted. Only a few of the DAs adopted the general manager and the innovator role, and it was the role of administrator with its characteristics of servicing and maintaining on which most DAs seemed to concentrate (Stewart, Smith, Blake and Wingate, 1980, p. 76).

Studies of the agendas of consensus management teams confirm a prevalence of non-strategic items, for example:

> In practice, few top managers are proactive in pursuit of these objectives (to provide services which are effective in improving health, comprehensive, accessible to all, responsive to the perceptions of users, and delivered in as efficient a manner as possible); they lack influence in relation to consultant staff (who are largely responsible for the pattern of health care services) and are in many cases reluctant to use the influence they do possess.
>
> (Schulz and Harrison, 1983, p. 52)

Proposition 3 Managers were reluctant to question the value of existing patterns of service, or to propose major changes in them

Studies show that incrementalism was a feature of planning and the allocation of resources at local level. Several studies characterize planning in the health service as 'what to do with the increment' (Glenerster, Korman and Marslen-Wilson, 1983, p. 264). David Hunter, in his study of the allocation of development funds in two Scottish health boards, noted there was always a tendency to seek more resources in preference to questioning the value of existing resource use. Development schemes, therefore, often meant 'more of the same'. He argued:

> At best, allocation of development funds, reflected a compromise between simply plugging the gaps in existing services, and ... initiating new services ... Often there was no choice ... Pressures from existing services presented officers with little or no alternatives but to plough more funds into them to relieve the pressures.
>
> (Hunter, 1980, p. 184)

Development lists were described by Hunter as 'shopping lists of deficiencies' (Hunter, 1979c, p. 627) and not linked to any broad development strategy. This, he argues, leads to policy stasis. In trying to explain this situation, Hunter stresses that, faced with a situation of complexity and uncertainty, people will rely on decision rules, rules of thumb or standard operating procedures, to make decision-making manageable. He cites a number of 'decision rules' or 'coping strategies' that were deployed by decision-makers in his study; these included seeking the answers to such questions: Who has done all right so far? Who has had too much in relation to the rest? Who has over/under spent? Who will it hurt least? A policy of appeasement or fair shares seemed to be favoured by administrators. Hunter argues that when considering the incremental approach to development fund allocations one needs to look for explanations, not only in terms of cognitive differences or insufficient information, or indeed technical problems, but also in terms of genuine puzzlement and uncertainty about what objectives the NHS ought to be pursuing. This uncertainty often leads to the pursuit of strategies and objectives that minimize risk, and seems to lead to effectiveness being measured in terms of improvements in the hotel aspects of the service, rather than impact on patient care or health.

Several studies note that planning was often seen as the exploration of what to do with hospital beds (Ham, 1981, p. 147; Glenester, Korman and Marslen-Wilson, 1983, p. 261; Rathwell, 1987). This reflects the power of the hospital consultants discussed earlier. It seems from existing studies that comment on the role of doctors in management that consultants' attitudes to planning health services tended to be framed by concerns such as 'my work', 'my beds' and 'my unit'.

Proposition 4   Managers behaved as if other groups of employees, rather than the public, were clients of the health service

The implication of this statement is that managerial behaviour is mainly producer-led rather than consumer-led. Studies which examine the involvement of the public in health services policy elaborate this point. Consumers in the NHS are formally represented by CHCs. Studies of CHCs confirm Harrison's proposition. CHCs were found to be polite and deferential (Hallas, 1976, p. 59), reluctant to use their powers (Klein and Lewis, 1976, p. 135), rarely consulted (Ham, 1980, p. 226) and were often labelled 'watchdogs without teeth' by the health service press.

Ham notes that the contribution which CHCs are able to make to NHS planning depends on the access to information they are granted. Despite having a right to basic information from health authorities, the annual reports of CHCs studied by Ham indicate that nearly all CHCs experienced difficulties in attempting to exercise this right. He goes on to point out that only rarely do health authorities deliberately withhold information. The major reason for poor involvement, according to Ham, is the time given for CHCs to contribute to planning (they are often asked for views at a late stage in the planning cycle) and the tendency of administrators not to place a high value on CHC participation (Ham, 1980, p. 226; Stewart *et al.*, 1980).

DISCUSSION OF THE RESEARCH FINDINGS FROM EMPIRICAL STUDIES OF NHS MANAGEMENT UP UNTIL 1983

The ethnographies of local health services summarized above are helpful in allowing one to peep into the black box of local health service management. These studies reveal that decisions affecting local health care delivery evolve in bargaining situations and that, although policy processes at a local level are incremental and plural, the distribution of power is weighted towards the medical profession. Several studies point to genuine uncertainty amongst health service managers as to how to prioritize the many demands on finite resources. This task is made more difficult by the absence of reliable information about the costs or benefits of various treatments, unclear central policy guidelines and the powerful emotional arguments marshalled by doctors in the name of clinical autonomy.

Yet, in spite of the usefulness of these studies in empirically demonstrating the dilemmas faced by health service managers and the actions of managers in the face of these dilemmas, such studies do not offer a convincing analysis of these findings. A number of explanations are offered for the relative failure of NHS management to meet changing health care needs. Cognitive differences between those managing health services is one such explanation, for example, the different training and socialization processes of doctors and administrators. Technical problems are also given as an explanation, for example poor information about health outcomes. Genuine puzzlement about what objectives the NHS should be pursuing is yet another explanation which hints at the failure of the government to provide a clear, consistent policy steer. Most explanations, however, centre on the inability of managers to challenge the long-established power of the medical profession. Notwithstanding such references to other groups within the health service, it may be argued that these explanations cannot be said to constitute a thoroughgoing sociological analysis because they do not adequately locate managers' actions in the social context (that is, the complex network of relationships) of which managers are a part. The complexity of these networks is often reduced so that managerial relationships are seen as relationships involving only those people with whom the management team or administrator has face-to-face contact. These points are developed later on in the book.

Another criticism one could make of this body of empirical research is the unwillingness of the researchers to consider the impact of health care management and health care reorganization on patient care and health. In this respect, researchers, like managers, could be accused of behaving as if other groups of employees rather than the public, were clients of the health service (Harrison's fourth proposition about health care management).

It is one thing to voice dissatisfaction with the analysis of these studies (recognizing their important contribution), it is another to offer an alternative. In my own research (Dopson, 1994) I found the approach of Norbert Elias helpful in dealing with some of the more theoretical issues involved in the analysis of 'managed social change'. The next chapter documents the key aspects of figurational or process sociology developed by Norbert Elias, as a prelude to applying this approach to some empirical problems relating to health service management.

3 Eliasian Sociology

INTRODUCTION

One is always aware of the dangers of being seduced by an attractive framework that one feels will assist in bringing order to chaotic empirical material. Nevertheless, Elias's approach is distinctively different from that of most other sociologists, and the possibility of applying some of Elias's ideas to the study of health care organization and management is in part the motivation for putting together this book. This chapter considers Elias's work and argues that, though his approach has not been applied to the analysis of health care organizations,[1] it has much to offer those involved in research in the area of NHS organization and management.

FIGURATIONAL OR PROCESS SOCIOLOGY

Figurational or process sociology, as Elias called his approach, is a minority standpoint amongst social scientists. Recently De Swaan has gone so far as to say that Elias is seen by many social scientists as eccentric, deserving, if not of being read and quoted, at least of highest praise, but wholly outside of the mainstream of academic social science (De Swaan, 1990, p. 4). He goes on to say he feels this is a 'fundamental error' since:

> Elias has confronted the central task of social science in the tradition of the classical authors, and his historical, sociological investigations into state formation and the civilizing process have pointed to a new course for mainstream social science to follow.
>
> (De Swaan, 1990, p. 4)

Goudsblom notes four themes of Elias's work which illustrate the principles of figurational or process sociology. They are:

1. Sociology is about people in the plural – human beings who are interdependent with each other in a variety of ways, and whose lives evolve in, and are significantly shaped by, the social

figurations they form together. People do not exist in a vacuum or in an asocial context.

2. These figurations are continually in flux, undergoing changes of many kinds – some rapid and ephemeral, others slower but perhaps more lasting.
3. The long-term developments taking place in human figurations have been, and continue to be, largely unplanned and unforeseen.
4. The development of human knowledge takes place within human figurations and is one important aspect of their overall development (Goudsblom, 1977, p. 105).

At the heart of Elias's sociology is a concern with the subject matter of sociology. Elias noted that many sociologists seek to investigate the behaviour, views and experience of individual people and then seek to process their results statistically. By focusing on component parts, sociologists hope to bring to light the characteristics of these composite units (Elias, 1970, p. 71). He attributed this approach in part to the influence of the classical tradition of the physical sciences and the belief that classical physics is the model to which all other scientific studies should look for guidance (Elias, 1969, p. 117). The classical tradition advocates that the way to investigate a composite unit is to dissect it into component parts, study the properties of the component parts in isolation and then, finally, to explain the distinguishing properties of the composite unit in terms of its component parts.

Elias took issue with this view and argued that the more closely integrated are the components of a composite unit, or the higher the degree of functional interdependence, the less possible it is to explain the properties of the latter in terms of the former. In such a case it becomes necessary not just to explore a composite unit in terms of its component parts (analysis), but also to explore the way in which these individual components are bonded to each other so as to form a composite unit (synthesis).

A study of the configuration of the unit parts, or, in other words, the structure of the composite unit, becomes a study in its own right. This is the reason why sociology cannot be reduced to psychology, biology or physics: its field of study – the figurations of interdependent human beings – cannot be explained if one studies human beings singly. In many cases the opposite procedure is advisable – one can understand many aspects of the behaviour or actions of individual people only if one sets out from the study of the pattern of their interdependence, the structure of their societies, in short from the figurations they form with each other.

(Elias, 1970, p. 72)

For Elias, it was the interdependencies between people – in his terms figurations – which provide sociology with its field of study. According to Elias, figurations are best thought of not simply as congeries of particular individuals known by name, but also as impersonal and, to some extent, self-regulating, self-perpetuating configurations (Elias, 1970, p. 56). It follows, therefore, that people are interdependent with others whom they have never met, and can therefore be affected by the activities of others whom they have never met. For example, a fundamental constraint on the career structure of NHS managers is provided by government decisions. Elias believed that because of the conventional, dichotomous approach to thinking about the individual and society, sociologists have been trapped in unproductive arguments about whether society or the individual is more real and which should come first as a point of departure in sociological investigation. Furthermore Elias argues that much of sociology has been based on an egocentric model of society (see Figure 3.1) in which the isolated static individual or ego stands at the centre of a series of concentric circles, the first being me, with my family, with my workplace, my town, my country, and a succession of ever-wider zones beyond (Elias, 1970, p. 14).

Very few sociologists, Elias argued, have attempted to break away from this egocentric conception. Weber, whilst fully aware that individuals were steeped in the social, nevertheless 'axiomatically' believed in the 'absolute individual' ... as the true social reality. (Elias, 1970, p. 117). Concepts like 'state', 'family', 'army' or 'class', were seen by him as simply a particular pattern in individual people's social action. Mennell has recently argued that this led Weber into such absurdities as arguing that private prayer, an accidental collision between cyclists, or many people simultaneously putting up umbrellas when it rained, are not instances of social action – as if praying or riding a bicycle, or using an umbrella were activities that could be understood independently from the social development of religion and technology (Mennell, 1989, p. 255).

Similar problems, argued Elias, beset Talcott Parsons's voluntaristic theory of action. Parsons begins from the model of interaction between two people, referred to as ego and alter (Parsons, 1951). Mennell argues:

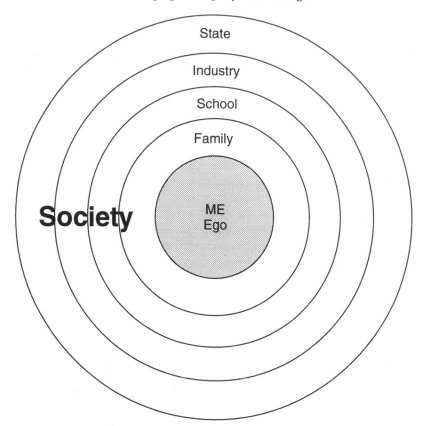

Figure 3.1   An egocentric model of society
Source: Elias, 1970, p. 14.

It is highly significant that in this famous didactic model, not only
'ego', but also 'alter' – the 'other person' – is conceptualized as a
single, isolated entity, rather than a multiplicity of other people,
directly or indirectly, interdependent with 'ego' and with each other.
(Mennell, 1989, p. 255)

Elias argued that Durkheim struggled valiantly with the chicken and
egg problems raised by what Elias termed *homo clausus* (man or
woman as an isolated static individual) assumptions (Durkheim,
1938), but still fell prey to making society appear something existing
over and above individuals, surrounding and penetrating them, and

therefore still bowed to the assumption that society and the individual can best be conceptualized as separate things.

Elias also pointed to the trend in sociology to reduce processes conceptually to a static state in the name of analysis. He noted that much of our everyday language does the same:

> Our languages are constructed in such a way that we can often only express constant movement or constant change, in ways which imply that it has the character of an isolated object at rest, and then, almost as an afterthought, adding a verb which expresses the fact that the thing with this character is now changing. For example, standing by a river we see the perpetual flowing of the water, but to grasp it conceptually, and to communicate it to others, we do not think to say, 'look at the perpetual flow of the water'; we say, 'look how fast the river is flowing' We say 'the wind is blowing', as if the wind were actually a thing at rest, which, at a given point in time, begins to move and blow. We speak as if the wind was separate from its blowing, as if a wind could exist which did not blow. And this reduction of processes to static conditions, which we shall call 'process reduction', for short, appears self explanatory to people who have grown up with such language. They often imagine it is impossible to think and speak differently, but that is simply not so. Linguists have shown that many languages have structures which make it possible to assimilate such experiences differently.
> (Elias, 1970, pp. 111–12)

Elias passionately believed that sociology needed to find a new means of speaking and thinking:

> At first it might perhaps seem that an effort to reorient our thinking might complicate the work of sociology. But the reverse is true. If this effort is made, the work becomes simpler. The complexity of many modern sociological theories is due, not to the complexity of the field of investigation which they seek to elucidate, but the kind of concepts employed. These may be concepts which either have proved their worth in other (usually physical) sciences, or are treated as self-evident in every-day usage, but which are not at all appropriate to the investigation of specifically social functional nexuses.
> (Elias, 1970, p. 111)

It was Elias's view that one of the most promising models for non-reifying concept formation found in our everyday language is personal pronouns. Personal pronouns, he argued, represent the elementary set of coordinates by which all human groupings can be plotted out (Elias, 1970, p. 123):

> The function of the pronoun 'I' in human communication can only be understood in the context of all the other positions to which the other terms in the series refer. The six other positions are absolutely inseparable, for one cannot imagine an 'I' without a 'he', or a 'she', a 'we', 'you' (singular and plural) or 'they'.   (Elias, 1970, p. 123)

Elias argued that, taken together, personal pronouns are an elementary expression of the fact that every person is fundamentally related to other people and that every human individual is therefore fundamentally a social being. Using personal pronouns leads to an easy transition from the image of man or woman as *homo clausus* to one of *homines aperti*[2] (people in the plural) – and also helps us to understand that the concept 'individual' refers to interdependent people in the singular and the concept of society to interdependent people in the plural. The first field, he believed, ought to be the concern of psychologists and psychiatrists, the second of sociologists and social-psychologists.

Elias argued that by adopting his view of the scope of sociology, sociologists can move away from parochial specialist models of man, the best known of which is *homo economicus*, but which are refined versions of *homo clausus*, the dominant concept of man or woman in contemporary industrial society (Elias, 1969, p. 122).

Elias drew on the word 'figuration' because it was a more dynamic and processual term and highlighted the inadequacies of the existing static vocabulary of sociologists:

> Looking through sociology textbooks, one finds many technical terms which convey the impression of referring to isolated and motionless objects; yet on closer scrutiny they refer to people who are or were constantly moving and constantly relating to other people. Think of concepts like norm and value, structure and function, social class or social system. The very concept of society has this character of an isolated object in a state of rest, and so has that of nature. The same goes for the concept of the individual. Consequently we always feel impelled to make quite senseless conceptual distinctions, like 'the individual and society' which makes it seem that 'the individual' and 'the society', were two separate things, like

tables and chairs or pots and pans. One can find oneself caught up in long discussions of the nature of the relationship between these two apparently separate objects. Yet, on another level of awareness, one may know perfectly well that societies are composed of individuals, and that individuals can only possess specifically human characteristics, such as their abilities to speak, think, and love, in and through their relationships with other people – 'in society'.

(Elias, 1970, p. 113)

If one accepts that we live in a social context, that is to say we live within and are part of a network of social relationships, the question then arises, what is a relationship? There is a pervasive tendency for people, particularly citizens of western society with their emphasis on individualism, to conceive of relationship in terms of face-to-face contacts. This view is entirely understandable and based on the often unspoken assumption that the people with whom one has most contact are bound to have the greatest impact on us. While no-one would deny the influence of those closest to us, to adopt this view places an unnecessary limitation on the concept of relationship. People all over the world are constantly engaged in activities which affect the lives of other people of whose existence they are often oblivious. When we speak of relationships it is important to understand these in terms of global networks. In other words, while we may feel many of the effects of relationships, there are also some effects which impact upon us without us being aware of them. An example of the way in which we are capable of internalizing a mode of behaviour without being consciously aware of the process is provided by the way in which we sleep. In western societies at least, infants tend to be transferred from cots to beds around the age of two. Initially, many youngsters have a tendency to respond to this less restricted environment by falling out of bed. Gradually, even though they are asleep, they learn to toss and turn in bed and yet remain within its bounds. Beds are social products. Their dimensions have been established by fellow human beings and adults have learnt to accept their limitations without giving them a second thought. This is quite a remarkable process because it provides an example of the way in which social mores can influence us even when we are in a state of unconsciousness.[3]

We as individual people have been, and continue to be, influenced by the activities of past generations. Not only have we inherited from them material things like buildings, roads and so on, but also less tangible things like language, political ideologies and religious beliefs. Successive generations – whether they intended it or not – have passed on the social world they inherited and which they modified during the course of their lives. Elias's book, *The Civilizing Process* (Elias, 1939), is an illuminating demonstration of how normative practice can be passed down over hundreds of years even though, in the process, the vast majority of people remain oblivious of its origins. This work highlights the weakness of any perspective which assumes that all behaviour can be understood adequately in terms of conscious processes, or in terms simply of the here-and-now.

Central to Elias's concept of figuration is the closely related concept of power chances or balance of power. That is, people are interdependent, but they are not necessarily equally interdependent. The more dependent individuals are on others, the less power chances they have and *vice versa*:

> Where the balances of power within the web of interdependence are relatively equal, the web constrains the activities of those enmeshed in it, even more, and more evenly for all. The more extensive the web, the more probable it is that even the more powerful will be constrained by ambivalence, knowing that an uninhibited pursuit of their own desires could jeopardize the very links in the web on which they depend, bringing forth consequences which even they must fear.   (Mennell, 1989, p. 95)

Because people are differentially interdependent, the balance of power tends to be unequal. However, it is important to recognize that no groups – not even the most powerful groups – are all-powerful, for they are inevitably dependent to some degree on other less powerful groups.

Mennell notes that by the late 1980s, Elias had become irritated by the term 'figurational sociology' as a label applied to his own work and that of others influenced by him (Mennell, 1989, p. 251). He was concerned because figuration had become a label for another 'school' of sociological thought and, perhaps more importantly, he was also concerned that figuration was being used in just as static and reifying a way as 'social system'. He preferred the term 'process sociology' to describe his work because process is such an ordinary word and is therefore less susceptible to use as a 'cordon sanitaire' with which to quarantine his ideas.

THE METHODOLOGY APPROPRIATE TO PROCESS SOCIOLOGY

As well as commenting on the subject matter of sociology, Elias offers views on how to conduct research. There has been much debate about a methodology appropriate to sociology, often considered under the term 'philosophy of science' (see Popper, 1968; Medawar, 1969; Lakatos and Musgrave, 1970; Hanson, 1975; Barnes, 1982). The problem of involvement and detachment lies at the heart of a number of debates in the social sciences. Most commonly, the discussion has been framed in terms of a static polarity between 'objectivity' and 'subjectivity'. Elias suggested that one of the problems with concepts like 'objectivity' and 'subjectivity' – concepts which are perhaps more characteristic of a philosophical rather than of a properly sociological approach to problems of knowledge – is that they tend to suggest a static and unbridgeable divide between two entities, 'subject' and 'object', as though these were 'two inert figures standing at a distance from each other at opposite sides of a great divide' (Elias, 1987, p. 112). Closely associated with this is the almost ubiquitous tendency, among those who use these terms, to describe research in all-or-nothing terms, that is to describe it as either totally 'objective' or, conversely, as completely lacking objectivity, that is, as being 'subjective' in an absolute sense.

Furthermore, Elias argued, it is not possible in these terms adequately to describe the development of modern science, for this development was a long-term process, and there was not a single historic moment when objective, scientific knowledge suddenly emerged, fully formed, out of what had formerly been wholly subjective forms of knowledge. Elias argued that what is required is more adequate conceptualization of our ways of thinking about the world, and of the processes as a result of which our present ways of thinking about the world have come about. Elias's conceptualization of the problem in terms of degrees of involvement and detachment is, in my view, more adequate than conventional arguments because, firstly, it does not involve a radical dichotomy between categories such as 'objective' and 'subjective', as though these were mutually exclusive categories; and, secondly, because this conceptualization is both relational and processual. It allows social scientists to make statements about the changing relationships between 'objects' and 'subjects', whether the objects be in the 'natural' world or the 'social' world, and it provides us with a framework with which we can examine the development, over time, of more scientific (or what Elias called more object-adequate or alternatively more reality-congruent) knowledge.

In elaborating on his conceptualization of degrees of involvement and detachment, Elias emphatically denied the possibility that the outlook of any sane adult can be either wholly detached or wholly involved. Normally, he noted, adult behaviour lies on a scale somewhere between these two extremes:

> One cannot say of a man's outlook in any absolute sense that it is detached or involved (or, if one prefers, 'rational' or 'irrational', 'objective' or 'subjective'). Only small babies, and among adults perhaps only insane people, become involved in whatever they experience with complete abandon to their feelings here and now; and again only insane people can remain totally unmoved by what goes on around them.   (Elias, 1956, p. 226)

Thus the concepts of involvement and detachment 'do not refer to two separate classes of objects . . . what we observe are people and people's manifestations, such as patterns of speech or of thought . . . some of which bear the stamp of higher, others of lesser detachment or involvement' (Elias, 1987, p. 4). Clearly, therefore, Elias is not suggesting that it is possible for us to obtain 'ultimate truth', or complete detachment. Some critics of figurational sociology have alleged that advocates of this approach claim to be able to offer 'objective' analyses of social processes. From what has been said, it should be clear that this was never Elias's position and, indeed, it is a position which he explicitly rejected.

Elias noted that sociologists, like everyone else, are members of many social groups outside of their academic communities – families, clubs, political parties and so on – and they cannot cease to take part in, or to be affected by, the social and political affairs of their groups and their time. In this sense, they cannot be wholly detached. However, Elias goes on to note that there is at least one sense in which it would not be desirable, in terms of the development of sociology, for them to be wholly detached, even if this were possible. For while one need not know, in order to understand the structure of a molecule, what it feels like to be one of its atoms, in order to understand the way in which human groups work one needs to know from 'inside' how human beings experience their own and other groups, and one cannot know this without active participation and involvement. The problem for sociologists, then, is not the problem of how to be completely detached, but of how to maintain an appropriate balance between these two roles of everyday participant and scientific inquirer and, as a professional group, to establish in their work the undisputed dominance of the latter.

The question then arises of how it is possible to determine the position of specific attitudes or ways of thinking on this involvement/detachment continuum. In other words, how can we differentiate between attitudes or knowledge which reflect a relatively high degree of involvement, and those which reflect a higher degree of detachment? Why should we, as sociologists, seek to achieve a higher degree of detachment in our work? And what are the processes which, over a long period of time and as part of the process of social development, have gradually enabled people to think, first about the 'natural' world, and then, more slowly, about the 'social' world, in more detached terms? These questions can be best explored *via* a consideration of Elias's essay 'The Fishermen in the Maelstrom' (see Elias, 1956).

Elias begins his essay by retelling an episode from Edgar Allen Poe's famous story about the descent into the maelstrom. Two brothers who were fishermen were caught in a storm and were slowly being drawn into a whirlpool. At first, both brothers – a third brother had already been lost overboard – were too terrified to think clearly and to observe accurately what was going on around them. Gradually, however, the younger brother began to control his fear. While the elder brother remained paralysed by his fear, the younger man collected himself and began to observe what was happening around him, almost as if he were not involved. It was then that he became aware of certain regularities in the movement of objects in the water which were being driven around in circles before sinking into the whirlpool. In short, while observing and reflecting, he began to build up an elementary 'theory' relating to the movement of objects in the whirlpool. He came to the conclusion that cylindrical objects sank more slowly than objects of any other shape, and that smaller objects sank more slowly than larger ones. On the basis of his observations and of his elementary 'theory', he took appropriate action. While his brother remained immobilized by fear, he lashed himself to a cask and, after vainly encouraging his brother to do the same, leapt overboard. The boat, with his brother in it, descended rapidly into the whirlpool. However, the younger brother survived, for the cask to which he had lashed himself sank much more slowly, and the storm eventually blew itself out before the cask was sucked down into the whirlpool.

The story of the fishermen points up very clearly a kind of circularity – Elias also referred to it as a physio-psychological and socio-psychological double-bind – which is by no means uncommon in the development of human societies. Both brothers found themselves involved in processes – a storm and the associated whirlpool – which appeared wholly beyond their control. Not surprisingly, their emotional involvement in their situation paralysed their reactions, making it difficult for them to analyse what was happening to them, or to take effective action to maximize their chances of survival. Perhaps for a time they may have clutched at imaginary straws, hoping for a miraculous intervention of some kind. After a while, however, one of the brothers began, to some degree, to calm down. As he did so, he began to think more coolly. By standing back, by controlling his fear, by seeing his situation as it were from a distance – in other words, by seeing himself and his situation in a rather more detached way – he was able to identify certain patterns within the whirlpool. Within the general uncontrollable processes of the whirlpool, he was then able to use his new-found knowledge of these patterns in a way which gave him a sufficient degree of control to secure his own survival. In this situation, one sees very clearly that the level of emotional self-control, of detachment, and the levels of process control and of the development of more 'realistic' knowledge are all interdependent and complementary.

This same kind of circularity can also be seen in the reaction of the older brother, who perished in the whirlpool. High exposure to the dangers of a process tends to increase the emotivity of human responses. High emotivity of response lessens the chance of a realistic understanding of the critical process and, hence, of a realistic practice in relation to it. In turn, relatively unrealistic practice under the pressure of strong emotional involvement lessens the chance of bringing the critical process under control. In short, inability to control tends to go hand in hand with high emotivity of response, which minimizes the chance of controlling the dangers of the process, which keeps at a high level the emotivity of the response, and so forth.

Insofar, therefore, as we are able to control our emotional involvement with the processes we are studying, we are more likely to develop a more realistic or 'reality-congruent' analysis of those processes. Conversely, the more emotionally involved we are, the more likely it is that our strong emotional involvement will distort our understanding. It is this consideration which constitutes the primary rationale for Elias's argument that we should seek, when engaged in research, to obtain the highest level of detachment. He describes this as a 'detour *via* detachment'.

What this means is not that we should cease to be concerned about solving practical problems which concern us but that, at least for the duration of the research, we try, as sociologists, to put these practical and personal concerns to one side, in order that we can study the relevant processes in as detached a manner as possible. A relatively detached analysis is more likely to result in a relatively realistic or object-adequate analysis, and this in turn will provide a more adequate basis for the formulation of relevant policy. In contrast, policy which is formulated in a highly emotionally charged situation, and where the policy-makers feel under political or other pressure to 'do something', is rather less likely to be based on a cool, calm and reflective – in short, a relatively detached – examination of the situation.

It is the case that some individuals are more able than others to adopt a relatively detached perspective when making observations about either the 'natural' or the 'social' world. Usually, for example, adults are able to be more detached about the world around them than are children. It is also the case that some adults – for a variety of reasons – find it easier than others to adopt a relatively detached perspective. Notwithstanding these variations between one individual and another, it was a fundamental point of Elias's argument that the development of more object-adequate forms of knowledge, and the associated development of more detached perspectives in the sciences, have to be understood as social processes, that is, as aspects of changing patterns of interdependence, of figurations.

Elias noted that the processes which facilitate what he called a 'detour *via* detachment' are more firmly established in the physical and biological sciences than in the social sciences. For example, medical scientists may have a strong commitment, perhaps based on religious or humanitarian convictions, to reducing human pain and suffering, but this does not prevent them, in their capacity as scientists, from studying biological processes with a relatively high degree of detachment. The level of detachment characteristic of the perspective of physical scientists such as physicists or astronomers is probably even more pronounced. How, then, do we account for the differing levels of detachment which are characteristic of the different sciences? Can these differences be explained in terms of the intrinsically different characteristics of objects in the physical, the biological and the social worlds? Is it inherently easier to be relatively detached about natural than about social processes? And how does one account for the fact that people in more complex societies tend, on the whole, to adopt a rather more detached perspective in relation to the world around them than do people in less complex societies? Elias argues that a more adequate understanding of these issues can be developed if we adopt a processual or developmental model such as that provided by figurational sociology.

People living in pre-scientific societies are, to a much greater extent than those in scientific societies, exposed to the blind vagaries of nature, including their own. Their capacity for controlling, and therefore for protecting themselves from, unwelcome natural processes such as floods or storms is comparatively limited. In contrast, the members of more developed societies enjoy the benefit of a vast social fund of knowledge. The rapid growth of knowledge in the last four or five hundred years has meant that the fund of knowledge available to people living in the modern-day scientific societies has become both more comprehensive and, at least with regard to the non-human levels, more realistic or more reality-congruent – that is, more congruent with the factual course of events than with the promptings of people's wishes, fears and the fantasies associated with them. In conjunction with this growth in knowledge, what Elias called the 'safety area' which people build for themselves, that is the area amenable to their control, has become very much larger than it used to be. As a consequence, people in those societies are now able, at least in certain areas, to steer their way through the flow of blind and unmanageable processes better than their forebears – at least at the physical levels, if less so at the human levels, just as people aboard ships are able to steer their way through the unmanageable waters of the oceans.[4]

This growth in the social fund of knowledge has, then, enabled people in more developed societies to expand their control within the uncontrollable flow of events, thus providing themselves with a 'protective shell' which helps to keep out the dangers emanating from the non-human levels of the overall process.[5] However, even in the most developed of societies, in which a scientific approach is most highly institutionalized, people have not yet developed an equally comprehensive and realistic fund of knowledge relating to social processes, that is, to the way humans behave towards and relate with each other. As a consequence, they do not have the same degree of control in relation to social processes – and perhaps most notably in relation to the dangers which humans constitute for each other, for example in terms of war and other forms of conflict – as they have in relation to many natural processes. In that respect the double-bind situation, in which low ability to control dangers and a high fantasy-content of knowledge reinforce each other, still prevails to a considerable degree in relation to social processes, even in the most developed societies.

Elias points out that people living in more developed societies usually take for granted the vast social fund of scientific knowledge which they have inherited. Rarely, for example, do they try to imagine what it was like to cope without the necessities of life and to struggle for survival equipped with a fund of knowledge which was much smaller and much less certain than that to which they have access in their daily lives. Indeed, many people living in developed societies appear to believe that the lower fantasy-content and greater realism of their knowledge are due, not to the fact that they live in relatively highly developed societies, but to some superior personal qualities – of 'rationality', or 'civilization' – which they possess by virtue of their own nature and which people in earlier or less developed societies did not or do not possess, or possess only in smaller doses. They might describe such people as 'superstitious' or 'irrational', which they may regard as an explanation but which, in fact, explains nothing. It simply means: 'We are better'. Such a claim is, of course, quite wrong, for we cannot take any personal credit from the fact that we happen to have been born into a society in which scientific modes of thinking have been institutionalized to a relatively high degree.

In order to understand something of the way in which human knowledge has developed, it is important to understand that people living in earlier and relatively simple societies could not possibly have thought in the same way that we do, for they had not inherited the results of a more or less rapid growth of knowledge over hundreds of years, and their social fund of knowledge, and especially the knowledge of what we call 'nature', was very much smaller than ours. Their standard modes of thinking were, to a much greater extent, permeated by their own wishes and fears. They were to a greater extent geared to fantasies, both of a collective and of an individual kind. Because of their smaller and less reality-congruent fund of knowledge, their capacity for controlling the dangers to which they were exposed – and also for controlling their own destiny – was also smaller. Greater, therefore, was the insecurity in which they lived and greater, too, was their concern with questions like 'What does it mean for me or for us?', and 'Is it good or bad for me or for us?' The questions they asked were more self-centred, and involved higher levels of affectivity of all experiences, all concepts and operations of thinking. The strength and depth of people's involvement in all events which, in their view, could affect their lives, left little room for concern with those problems characteristic of a higher level of detachment and emotional restraint – with questions such as 'What is it, and how has it come about?' and 'What is it *per se*', independently of 'What it means for me or for us?'

Elias's work offers a genuinely sociological theory of knowledge which does not assume that one can understand the way knowledge develops without reference to human emotions. In particular, his analysis of double-bind processes, in which relative inability to control critical processes is associated with high emotivity, with low levels of detachment and with explanations characterized by low levels of reality-congruence, enables us better to understand the different levels of detachment characteristic of the natural and the social sciences and, in examining the development of science as a social process, it also takes us considerably beyond what is a relatively sterile debate couched in dichotomous terms such as 'objectivity versus subjectivity'.

As for the loosening of the double-bind process, the simple example of the fishermen in the maelstrom does not of itself provide an instant solution, but it does point us, at least some way, in the direction of a solution. Simply to increase our understanding and our awareness of these problems of involvement and detachment, and of the nature of double-bind circularities, may be of some assistance in breaking into the double-bind process, and thereby easing the constraint which this kind of process puts upon people in thinking and in acting. Such a process is a long and slow and difficult process, not least because the development of more object-adequate knowledge may threaten deeply cherished beliefs. It is however, important that sociologists make an attempt to attain a greater degree of detachment, for only by doing so will they be in a position significantly to enhance our understanding of the social world.[6]

APPLICATIONS OF FIGURATIONAL OR PROCESS SOCIOLOGY

Various research themes have been inspired by Elias's work, and a great deal of effort has gone into applying the theory of the civilizing process into areas not covered by Elias (Wouters, 1986; De Swaan, 1988). Another common theme relates to the continuation of the state formation process in the nineteenth and twentieth centuries, which raises questions about the modern welfare state and its implications for personality structure (Wouters, 1982; De Swaan, 1988). However as Kranendonk points out in his bibliography of figurational sociology in the Netherlands:

> Research teams tend to range widely, as they do in Elias's own work, with regard to time, space and to topic. By and large, the linking characteristics are rather to be found in the general approach, in the use and avoidance of particular concepts and terms of phrase, and the style which tends to be more literary and polished than the average standard in sociology.
>
> (Kranendonk, 1989, p. 21)

Very little has been written about organizational conflict and change within an Eliasian framework and nothing specifically on managerialism and the NHS. As a result of a literature search and conversations with academics working in the tradition of Eliasian sociology, I discovered four pieces of work broadly considering organizational issues, namely Dunning and Sheard's study of 'The Bifurcation of Rugby Union and Rugby League' (1976), De Swaan's study of the welfare state (1988), Ivan Waddington's study of the campaign for medical registration in Britain (1984) and a series of consultancy techniques based on the sociology of Elias written by Mastenbroek (1987). These studies have in common a commitment to get behind the institutional facade at various stages of the organization's history. They consider institutions as part of a wide figuration or network of ever-changing human relationships. At this point in the book it is helpful to pause and consider what, in general terms, figurational or process sociology can offer those studying the organization and management of the NHS and those charged with planning and managing change in health services.

Firstly, one is made aware of the limitations of viewing the NHS simply as an organization which has been purposefully constructed or structured in order to pursue specific goals. The NHS in its present form is the result of a number of complex social processes (see Chapter 2 for a flavour of that complexity) and, like other organizations, the NHS has fallen, and will invariably fall, prey to what Merton has called unanticipated consequences of purposive social actions (Merton, 1936). Indeed the development of the NHS is itself almost certainly part of what Elias calls 'blind processes', that is:

Human beings may not be aware of the figuration of which they are a part, of the nature of prevailing interdependencies, and therefore may ignore or misunderstand the results of their actions. It is because of these unintended consequences of human actions that developments may occur as a 'blind process'.

(De Swaan, 1990, p. 7)

It is not, therefore, appropriate to view either of the two reorganizations of the NHS discussed earlier simply as rational attempts to meet the single goal of improving the way in which health services are delivered. Because of the sheer complexity and dynamic nature of the relational network which is called the NHS, the resulting interactions generate a whole series of unintended consequences or outcomes. In a real sense, each reorganization could be said to be an attempt to deal with the unintended consequences or outcomes of the formation and earlier development of the NHS. Therefore to begin to understand developments in the organization of the NHS, it is important to avoid conceiving the NHS as a social structure which is separate from and constraining upon, the people who work within it. Elias urges us to see social structure as the network of relationships themselves. These networks are not something separate from the social life of the people who make up the network, but these networks are these people in their interrelationship. Moreover the NHS is not a static organization, but a process. A more sociological view of organizations is developed by Dunning and Sheard who, drawing on Elias, see organizations as:

Configurations of interdependent human beings who have been socialized into the norms and values of a given culture, perhaps into those of a given specific sub-culture. Moreover, the personnel, at least in complex societies, have multiple memberships and hence, very often, conflicting allegiances. They also tend to be subjected to conflicting pressures. As a result, no organization can ever be insulated from the wider society within which it is set. Organizations, that is to say, do not have impermeable boundaries. Even 'total institutions' are not completely closed, but have relations of various kinds with the outside world.

(Dunning and Sheard, 1976, p. 35)

Secondly, an Eliasian perspective helps make one aware of the flaw in the literature on the NHS that speaks of the failure of the organization of the NHS to meet the goals of the NHS. To pursue this line of argument ignores the fact that while individuals have goals, organizations do not. Only individual members of organizations can have goals, for as Dunning and Sheard point out:

> To think of organizational goals is to involve the reification of the concept of organization and renders it 'consensualist' and 'harmonistic'. (Dunning and Sheard, 1976, p. 33)

Thirdly, Elias alerts us to the point that figurations, including organizations, which are a particular type of figuration, are complex networks of social relationships, and cannot be adequately conceived simply as face-to-face contacts. Many of the studies of health care management which focus on the relationships of the various groups within the NHS make this assumption. As noted earlier this reflects the pervasive tendency for people, perhaps particularly citizens of western societies with their emphasis on individualism, to conceive of relationships in terms of face-to-face contacts. However, this is a dangerous assumption. For example, government ministers have far more influence on our lives than do many people whom we meet regularly in face-to-face contact. People working within the NHS have relationships with people they have never met and, indeed, they are affected by relationships of which they may be more or less unaware. In addition these relationships are inexorably linked to past generations of NHS workers in a variety of ways, for example, the power of doctors today can only be understood in terms of the actions of past generations of doctors. Not only have present day NHS workers inherited material things, such as the preponderance of hospitals as a centre for providing care, but also less tangible things such as language, methods of working, the division of labour in health care and so on. People working within an organization such as the NHS often internalize norms in an unquestioning way, and, as a consequence, researchers cannot assume that all behaviour within the organization can be adequately understood simply in terms of conscious processes.

Fourthly, although many of the studies of local health services management have correctly drawn our attention to the relatively powerful position of doctors, Elias reminds us not to fall into the trap of assuming that doctors are all-powerful in the sense that they wield absolute power. Even the most powerful group's attempts to achieve their goals are always mediated by other groups, whether or not the participants are aware of this.

Fifthly, Eliasian sociology highlights the futility of the search for single causes. They are too simplistic though this is, of course, their attraction. In order to understand social processes, it is not sufficient to focus upon individuals or on the subjective perceptions of individuals (as does much of the existing literature on health care management). We need to focus on the emerging network of relationships which involves both the intended and unintended consequences of human action. If it were possible to understand social development solely in terms of the motives and meanings of individuals, then there would be no need for a sociological perspective for we would simply have to talk to the participants about their intentions. It is the unintended consequences or outcomes flowing from complex human interactions which make a sociological perspective imperative.

Using the implementation of the Griffiths Report as an example, the next two chapters examine the way in which sociologists and others have examined the process of managing change within the NHS. Several studies of Griffiths have documented a number of unintended consequences of its implementation, but it is argued that none of these has adequately theorized these unintended outcomes of the policy implementation process. It is suggested that the process-sociological approach of Norbert Elias, and in particular his game models, enable us better to understand the complex interweaving of planned and unplanned processes which is involved in all processes of managed change.

4 The Introduction of General Management in the NHS: An Example of Managed Social Change

INTRODUCTION

As has been discussed, until 1984 the NHS had two unusual organizational characteristics: the national uniformity of its senior management structures, and the practice of 'consensus management'. Just as the dust of the NHS's second major reorganization was beginning to settle, what was seen by the government as the inability of the NHS management to achieve significant improvements in cost containment or unit management was cited by Minister Norman Fowler as evidence of the need for further change. Four leading businessmen were to conduct an independent management inquiry into the:

> ...effective use and management of manpower and related resources in the NHS from professional managers with experience in other large organizations.
> (DHSS 1983 NHS Management Inquiry; Press Release No. 83/30 3 February)

This chapter considers the details of this inquiry, known as the Griffiths Report. It examines the critique of the NHS as developed in this Report, the Griffiths recommendations for the NHS and the reactions to the Report from the various groups who work in the NHS. As an example of managed social change, the Griffiths Report offers an opportunity to explore the relevance of Eliasian or process sociology to understanding such processes of managed social change.

BACKGROUND TO THE GRIFFITHS REPORT

The Inquiry was led by Roy Griffiths, deputy chair and managing director of Sainsbury food stores. Other members of the team were:

Jim Blyth, group finance director of United Biscuits, Sir Brian Bailey, chair of Television South-West and Mike Bett, board member for personnel at British Telecom. The team also included a number of civil servants: Cliff Graham, a senior civil servant who was involved with the Rayner scrutinies on health care expenditure (1982), Kay Barton and Tim Stephens, who came to the Inquiry from the Permanent Secretary's office.

The government justified the selection of the Griffiths' team on the basis that each member had relevant expertise in meeting the needs of the public in very different ways (Barton, 1984). However, the selection of the team was a source of controversy. Davidman, for example, argues:

> What is completely missing from the Inquiry team is grass roots representation of any kind, from all those who would be affected by the Inquiry's findings, namely doctors, nurses, technical, ancillary staff, NHS patients, the community at large, the civil service, community health councils and trade unions.   (Davidman, 1984, p. 3)

Members of the Griffiths team were frequently reminded by the health service press that the NHS was not a supermarket or a biscuit chain. The inquiry team were sensitive to these criticisms, and attempted in the Report to clarify their remit:

> We were brought in not to be instant experts on all aspects of the NHS, but because of our business experience, to advise on the management of the NHS.
> (DHSS, 1983, hereafter referred to as The Griffiths Report, 1983, p. 10)

This argument is taken a stage further when the Report claims that the differences between the NHS and business in management terms, 'had been greatly overstated':

> The clear similarities between NHS management and business management are much more important. In many organizations in the private sector, profit does not immediately impinge on large numbers of managers below board level. They are concerned with levels of service, quality of product, meeting budgets, cost improvement, productivity, motivating and rewarding staff, research and development and 'long-term viability of the undertaking'.
> (The Griffiths Report, 1983, p. 10).

Within the nine-month limit set by the government for the Inquiry, the Griffiths team was given a free hand in how it collected the evidence. Rather than inviting evidence formally, the team was 'open to advice, invitations and written evidence'. Initially many of the invitations they were offered were accepted, but the team became increasingly selective, concentrating on the DHSS, unit level, regions and districts in that order (Barton, 1984). There was no detailed examination of the interactions between GPs, hospitals and community health services in providing health care. The Report itself does not include, as do for example Royal Commissions, a list of visits, nor a list of those who sent evidence for the Inquiry to consider.

As a general comment, the Inquiry team seemed more definite as to what it was not, rather than what it was. Its task was not: 'a manpower inquiry', 'a remit to change the statutory system or organizational financing of the NHS', 'a search for specific areas in which costs might be cut', 'a search for areas that might be contracted out to the private sector'; nor was it 'to cover Scotland, Wales and Northern Ireland' (The Griffiths Report, 1983, p. 24). It was definitely not intended to be a major addition to the already 'considerable library of the NHS literature'; rather the recommendations were shaped with an eye to the practicality of implementation (The Griffiths Report, 1983, p. 1). Therefore, for the sake of achieving actions on its own recommendations, the inquiry team decided not to suggest changes in legislation but confined itself to 'recommendations within the existing system' (The Griffiths Report, 1983, p. 2). This suggests that it is easier to achieve changes within the existing system rather than via legislation, a view contradicted by existing studies of local health care management discussed in Chapter 2.

It is interesting to note Sir Roy Griffiths' account of the background to setting up the Inquiry. In a guest lecture to the Audit Commission, he stated:

The background to the setting up of the Inquiry was the tremendous parliamentary questioning on the waste and inefficiency in the Service.[1] We were not at the outset asked to write a report, and the impression given was that we should simply advise at appropriate meetings, the whole exercise taking say a day a month for about eight months. Eight-and-a-half years and two days a week later I smile ruefully. Once we became involved, however, the noise level in the NHS reached almost unprecedented heights and Margaret Thatcher after three months requested that we should write something, however briefly, to encapsulate our observations and main recommendations. Since I and the other members were all working full-time for our respective companies we compromised by writing a 23 page letter to the Secretary of State simply saying without an exhaustive sweep of the options what we would do in his place.

(Griffiths, 1991, p. 2)

There are some interesting clues in this quotation about the assumptions in the Report and about the constraints under which the team worked which are discussed later.

THE GRIFFITHS CRITIQUE OF THE NHS

The Griffiths' Report, as the Inquiry became known, was published in October 1983. It takes the form of a letter to the Secretary of State and consists of recommendations for action as well as observations and some ten pages of background notes. Although brief, the Report sparked off a surge of interest, anxiety and controversy which has continued well after the Griffiths' postmortem.

The Report points to five areas of alleged weakness, documented in the 'Observations' section of the Report.

- A lack of strategic central direction.
- A lack of individual managerial responsibility.
- A failure to use objectives as a guide to managerial action.
- A neglect of performance.
- A neglect of the consumer.

(Hunter, Harrison, Marnoch and Pollitt, 1988, p. 1)

These criticisms are elaborated but not illustrated – still less validated – by various assertions scattered in the Report.

1. The NHS lacks strategic central direction

The Centre is still too much involved in too many of the wrong things and too little involved in some that really matter. For example, local management must be allowed to determine its own needs for information, with higher management drawing on that information for its own purposes. The units and the authorities are being swamped with directives without being given direction. Lack of the general management responsibility also means that certain major initiatives are difficult to implement.

(The Griffiths Report, 1983, p. 12)

2.   The service suffers from the absence of individual managerial responsibility which leads to 'lowest common denominator decisions'

If Florence Nightingale were carrying her lamp through the corridors of the NHS today, she would almost certainly be searching for somebody in charge.   · (The Griffiths Report, 1983, p. 12)

The absence of somebody in charge was illustrated by a summary of the complexity of the existing management process:

Management is currently provided by the Secretary of State and Minister of State, by the Permanent Secretary, and at regional and district level, by chairs appointed on a non-executive part-time basis... Management support is given at the Centre within the DHSS by senior officials and groups, none of whom is concerned full-time with the totality of NHS management; and at regional and district level by professional officers required to work in consensus management teams where each officer has the power of veto.

(The Griffiths Report, 1983, p. 11)

3.   The NHS fails to use objectives to guide managerial action, thus jeopardizing the implementation of plans and policies

... There is no driving force seeking and accepting direct and personal responsibility for developing management plans, securing their implementation and monitoring actual achievement. It means the process of devolution of responsibility, including discharging responsibility to the units, is far too slow...

To the outsider, it appears that when change of any kind is required, the NHS is so structured as to resemble a mobile, designed to move with any breath of air, but which in fact never changes its position and gives no clear indication of direction.

(The Griffiths Report, 1983, p. 12)

The failure of implementation was attributed in part to the process of consultation operating within the NHS, which by any business standards was thought to be:

... so labyrinthine and the rights of veto so considerable, that the
result in many cases is institution stagnation – a result particularly
enhanced by the fact that the machinery of implementation is
generally weak and, as such, cannot ensure that the processes of
consultation are effectively implemented and quickly brought to a
conclusion.   (The Griffiths Report, 1983, p. 14)

The assumption in these statements is that it is possible to change
organizations any way we wish, given the will to change.

**4.   The NHS does not have a performance orientation and is disinclined
to undertake economic or clinical evaluation, to collect the right kinds of
data or to be concerned with productivity**

The NHS does not have a profit motive, but it is, of course,
enormously concerned with the control of expenditure. Surprisingly, however, it still lacks any continuous evaluation of its performance against criteria.   (The Griffiths Report, 1983, p. 10)

The 'criteria' cited in the Report include levels of service, quality of
product, meeting budgets, cost improvement, productivity, and motiv-
ating and rewarding staff.

**5.   The NHS lacks a customer orientation, and is little concerned to
collect information about the views of NHS users**

Rarely are precise measurement objectives set; there is little measurement of health output; clinical evaluation of particular practices
is by no means common and economic evaluation of those practices
is extremely rare. Nor can the NHS display any ready assessment of
the effectiveness with which it is meeting the needs and expectations
of the people it serves. Businessmen have a keen sense of how well
they are looking after their customers. Whether the NHS is meeting
the needs of the patient, the community and can prove that it is
doing so, is open to question.   (The Griffiths Report, 1983, p. 10)

These criticisms imply that poor central management of the NHS has
led to piecemeal strategies and *ad hoc* interference in local management; and, secondly, that consensus management has failed in that the
requirement to 'get agreement' has overshadowed the need to make
decisions, resulting in long delays in the management process. All the

criticisms of the NHS made in the Report suggest that the NHS is being measured, not against private companies in the real world, but against an ideal – a typical model of how things 'ought' to be if only people would behave sensibly! It is difficult to imagine anything less sociological. Nonetheless, from these 'observations' a series of recommendations for the management of the NHS were put forward.

The general criticism of the lack of individual managerial responsibility was to be met by the introduction of general management defined in the Report as 'responsibility drawn together in one person, at different levels of the organization, for planning, implementation and control of performance' and the abandonment of formal consensus decision-making (The Griffiths Report, 1983, p. 11). General managers were to be 'the linchpin of dynamic management' and could be drawn from any discipline. The broad functions of the general manager are discussed in paragraphs 9 and 15 of the observation section of the Report. They were cast as chief executives, providing leadership and capitalizing on existing high levels of dedication and expertise amongst NHS staff of all disciplines. In addition, they were expected to stimulate 'initiative, urgency and vitality' amongst staff, to bring about a constant search for major change and cost improvement, to motivate staff and ensure that professional functions were effectively fed into the general management process.

It was carefully stated in the Report that the appointment of general managers was not intended to weaken the professional responsibilities of other chief officers '... especially in relation to decision-making on matters within their own spheres of responsibility' (The Griffiths Report, 1983, p. 17). The general manager was to be the final decision-taker for decisions normally in the province of consensus teams in the hope that delay and disagreement could be avoided. The chair of the health authority was given the task of 'clarifying the general management function and identifying a general manager for every unit of management' (The Griffiths Report, 1983, p. 6).

There were a number of proposals to meet the criticism of lack of objectives and poor implementation, namely: fixed contracts for general managers which were later rolling contracts; the creation of the NHS management board; the extension of the review process to unit level; and, later, individual performance review and performance-related pay.

Strengthening existing performance indicators (service performance targets devised to improve the use of resources, monitor quality and ensure accountability to the public) and developing a management budgeting approach (giving units/departments clearly-defined budgets, for which they are accountable) were regarded as vehicles for promoting the measurement of output in terms of patient care, and dealing with the criticisms that the NHS lacked a performance orientation. The regions were also to be strengthened as part of improving the performance orientation, although the nature of this process was not made clear.

Although doctors' involvement in management is intimately part of ensuring the NHS acquires a performance orientation, this was not explicitly tackled in the Report. Indeed the only mention of this critical aspect is on page 6 of the Report, where district and regional chairs are charged with, '... involving the clinicians more closely in the management process, consistent with clinical freedom for clinical practices'. Implicit in the Report is the hope that the development of budgets at unit level would involve clinicians and allow workload and service objectives to be related to financial and manpower allocations.

The Report stressed that patients and the community were to be the focus of the planning and delivery of services. To that end, health authorities were to ascertain, and act on, public opinion surveys and the advice of CHCs to ensure a consumer orientation for the NHS. The management board were made responsible for acting upon information regarding the experience and perceptions of patients in the community, given to them by the CHCs, market research and general practice, in formulating policy and monitoring performance against it (The Griffiths Report, 1983, p. 9).

An outline of the organizational structure proposed by Griffiths is given in Figure 4.1. The Secretary of State announced his acceptance of 'the general thrust' of the Report in his statement to the House of Commons on 25 October 1983, but added three caveats. Firstly, that the Report did not imply further statutory reorganization. He reiterated the point stressed by the Griffiths team regarding the need to 'enhance the best of consensus management'. All the recommendations, he said, were designed to take place within the existing statutory structure and without affecting the constitutional position of the patient, ministers or health authorities. Secondly, the recommendations should not add to the existing costs or staff numbers, and within the Department should lead to a reduction of activities and staff. Finally, the changes must ensure that the best deal for patients and the community was secured within available resources along with the best value for the taxpayer.

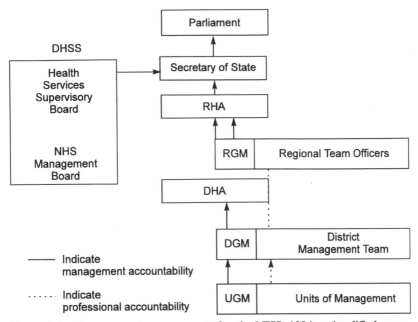

Figure 4.1 Management arrangements for the NHS, 1984: a simplified representation of future management relationships in health authorities and the DHSS

Source: The National Health Service Training Authority, *The New Management Arrangements for the NHS*, NHSTA, 1984.

As part of the House of Commons' statement, the Secretary of State announced he would be setting up within the Department the health services supervisory board. On 18 November 1983, he wrote to Health Authority chairs (Circular HC(84)13) to invite their views on two of the Griffiths recommendations: the general management function and the involvement of clinicians in the management process, asking for their views by 9 January 1984, so that implementation of general management could begin from April 1984.

REACTIONS TO THE GRIFFITHS RECOMMENDATIONS

A spectrum of reaction greeted the publication of the Report and its endorsement by the Secretary of State. For some, the introduction of general management was mainly a matter of seeking economies in what were thought to be over-elaborate and time-wasting practices associated with consensus management – 'cutting the administrative tail', as the Secretary of State put it at the time that the changes were being considered. Others, however, had greater expectations. General managers, they felt, should aim to achieve the transition from a passively administered to an actively managed service.

The eleven-week consultation period was the subject of much criticism. Before the consultation period ended, the House of Commons Social Services Committee began another Inquiry this time into the Griffiths recommendations. It held four public oral sessions, hearing evidence from the British Medical Association (BMA), the Association of Nurse Administrators (ANAs), the Health Visitors' Association (HVA), the Institute of Health Service Administrators (IHSA), the Association of Health Service Treasurers (AHST), the TUC Health Service Committee, the chair of regional chairs, the Nuffield Institute of Health Service Studies, Roy Griffiths and Sir Brian Bailey, the Secretary of State and his Permanent Secretary. It also invited three academic institutions to submit memoranda on the Report which were listed in the Annex. The Committee was not able to see responses from individual health authorities as the government had not laid them before the House of Commons. A brief summary of the evidence submitted to the Committee is given in Table 4.1.

Each of the responses to the Griffiths Report documented in Table 4.1 represents the standpoint of a particular managerial or professional group. The responses are unlikely to show the degree of detachment that one might expect from less involved groups (for example academics). This means that Table 4.1 should not be treated as objective analysis but as data and, in particular, as evidence of the complex interweaving of the multiplicity of interest groups that make up the NHS.

The Social Services Committee Report (published on 12 March 1984, some 20 days before what the Secretary of State had indicated was to be the implementation date) concluded that the reaction to the Griffiths Report had not been enthusiastic:

> It has been interpreted as an attack on NHS staff, as a threat to clinical freedom, a blow to nurse management... and a blueprint for reductions in the responsibilities of RHAs and DHAs and their members.   (Social Services Committee, 1984, paras 6 and 30)

However, the Committee welcomed the emphasis on the need to devolve management to the unit level and below, its proposed

Table 4.1 Inquiry into the Griffiths recommendations

Interest group	Key concerns following the Griffiths Report	Points of the Report accepted
Administrators	• Not enough discussion time • Understated progress made in implementing 1982 reorganization • Understated the importance of the coordinating role of the administrator • Unclear terms and conditions for general managers' post	• Need to improve the management process • Management budgeting for clinicians
Treasurers	• Appointments of general managers would be fair and equitable	• Better management was needed to bring about cost improvement and provide better value for money
Personnel	• Authorities would have freedom to organize management structures and appoint general managers fairly	• Backed need for a strong personnel director on the management board
Health Authority Members	• Health authorities ought to be free to make suitable local management arrangements • That the benefits flowing from consensus management would be lost • The role of the authority would be diminished in favour of the chair	• Need to improve managerial practice • Involvement of doctors more closely in management
Nurses	• There should be a nurse representative on the supervisory board • The role of nurses in management would be significantly diminished • The power of doctors would be increased • A curtailment of responsibility for the management of nursing	• Need for crisper management

Table 4.1   (*Contd*)

Interest group	Key concerns following the Griffiths Report	Points of the Report accepted
Public Health	• Lack of clarity about their own role	• Local flexibility for management relationships
Doctors	• Scrapping consensus management, which was seen as the most appropriate way to manage with professions • Role of medical advisory machinery	• Proposals for reform of the Centre • Doctors are natural managers
Para-professions	• Loss of professional input into management decisions • General managers could overturn professional decisions of departmental managers	• Improved management
Community Health Council	• Lack of clarification of the role of consumer groups in the decision-making process	
Unions	• Griffiths fails to tackle underfunding and inequalities in health	

extension of accountability reviews, and its search for more rigorous, efficient, consistent and sensitive management. More specifically, the Committee:

1. *Supported* the proposals for the DHSS and made the additional recommendation that a RHA chair and chief nursing officer should be members of the supervisory board and asked that the degree of managerial independence of the management board should be made known to the House of Commons (*ibid.*, para. 49);
2. *Recommended* that RHAs and DHAs should identify how their general management function is being performed, either within the present team structure by a nominated individual, or by the identification of a separate general manager (*ibid.*, para. 69);

3. *Recommended* that management at unit level should be considered separately from district and regional levels and should remain unchanged for the present (*ibid.*, paras 65 and 67);
4. *Wanted more information* about and elucidation of the evidence received by the Griffiths team, its proposals and responses to the 'consultative' letter of 18 November 1983, as well as the government's own interpretation of the recommendations (*ibid.*, para ??);
5. *Added its warning* that 'the NHS may suffer more in side-effects from the wonder-drug of general management than it gains in better management' (*ibid.*, para. 51).

The parliamentary debate on the Griffiths recommendations was held on 4 May 1984, and was not well-attended. At best, 20 MPs were present (see Russell, 1984). The Secretary of State rejected the Committee's caveats on general management at unit level, but accepted that the chief nursing officer should be a member of the supervisory board (*Hansard* 1984, Cols 642–6).

Arguing that the Griffiths recommendations did not constitute another major reorganizational upheaval for the NHS, the Secretary of State authorized publication of a DHSS Circular in June 1984

Table 4.2   Management appointments for the NHS, 1984

Previous post	Regional General Managers	District General Managers	Unit General Managers	Total
Administrator	9	113	347	469
Nursing officer	1	5	71	77
Consultant	–	4	82	86
Community physician	1	11	15	27
Treasurer	1	18	5	24
Dental officer	–	–	7	7
General practitioner	–	–	6	6
Professions allied to medicine	–	–	–	–
Ambulance driver	–	–	2	2
Other NHS	–	–	12	12
Other non-NHS	2	40	57	99
Vacancies	–	–	8	8
Totals	14	191	612	817

Source: Department of Health, Dec. 1986.

requiring health authorities to establish a general management function and to identify a general manager, first in RHAs, then DHAs
and, finally, at unit level. Membership of the management board was
finalized by April 1985.

By June 1985 most DGMs had been appointed, and by March 1987
most UGMs were in post. A breakdown of the general manager
appointments in England is given in Table 4.2.

REFLECTION ON THE REPORT'S FINDINGS

From the establishment of the Griffiths Inquiry team to the implementation of its key recommendations took less than two years. The
speed of implementation meant there was limited opportunity for
public debate, just as was the case with the 1974 reorganization
(Draper, Grenholm and Best, 1976, pp. 271–3).

The style of the Report, a letter of advice to the Secretary of State,
provided significantly less scope than usual for effective debate of
various reports in the House of Commons. The Social Services Committee commented that the proposals were so terse in their presentation that there was insufficient detail for critical analysis and many of
the Committee's recommendations were concerned with the need for
clarification of issues (*Griffiths Inquiry Report: Observations* 1984,
para. 52). Carrier and Kendall note:

> It is rare indeed for policy changes to follow the publication of a
> clearly written, thorough report which has been based on exemplary
> research, is subjected to extensive public consultation, and whose
> recommendations are first tried and tested in pilot projects before
> being adopted on a wider scale.
>
> (Carrier and Kendall, 1986, p. 209)

The Report's recommendations met none of the above criteria, indeed
they were based on a series of observations which could not be
logically deduced or empirically substantiated. For example, the case
against consensus management consisted of the phrase: 'Consensus
management leads to lowest common denominator decisions' which
contrasts with the Royal Commission's view that, although there were
some problems with consensus management, it was working well in
many areas and that there was general support for the principle
(*Royal Commission on the NHS*, 1979, p. 229). What public debate

there was had very little impact on the views of the Secretary of State. Indeed, the chair of the Social Services Committee, Renee Short, commented that he had 'ignored what we recommended... he has gone ahead and acted against the united medical, nursing and trade union opinion' (Russell, 1984, pp. 1546).

There are two explicit examples of the government's intention to accept the Griffiths recommendations, come what may. Firstly there was no public discussion about the restructuring of the DHSS. The decision to create the supervisory board was made some 19 days after the Griffiths team reported. Secondly, the letter of 8 February 1984, to health authorities, instructed them that the general management process would be introduced as from 1 April 1984. The letter was despatched four weeks before the Social Services Committee's Report and three months before the House of Commons debate.

In many senses, the Griffiths proposals were an act of faith, based on a report whose recommendations lack substantive evidence. The Report makes a number of important assumptions, which are discussed and challenged below:

1. *Politicians will deliver clear policies which general managers will implement.* This assumes politicians are aware of the complexities involved in providing health care and ignores the political capital politicians may make from the NHS which means that policy shifts can (and do) occur at any time and often reflect political rather than health care priorities.

2. *General management will not challenge existing arrangements for accountability.* Although the Secretary of State told the House of Commons that the new arrangements would not affect the constitutional position of Parliament, ministers and health authorities, the actual arrangements contradict this pledge in four major ways. Firstly, if the management board is to be allowed to manage, then Parliament must leave it space to do so and MPs must refrain from demands for detailed information about developments. With respect to this point, Day and Klein argue that the Report implies 'the NHS should be treated like a nationalized industry where members of Parliament may ask questions about overall performance but not raise specific cases or question specific decisions (Day and Klein, 1983, p. 1814). Secondly, the relationship of regional chairs to ministers must change, since, following Griffiths, they are now required to follow management directives from the management board. Thirdly, the Report

prescribes considerable independence for health authority chairs which potentially increases their power *vis-à-vis* their members and by implication must challenge accountability arrangements. Finally, an important question not addressed by the Report, is how the general management function would dovetail with professional structures. The Report is clear that the primary reporting relationship of functional officers is to the general manager, yet Figure 4.1 suggests that there will be a continuation of the functional relationship between districts and regions whereby the regional works officer relates directly to the district works officer, and so on.

3. *Private industry is more effectively managed than the public sector.* This is clearly open to question, given the relative efficiency of the NHS by comparison to other health care systems in the world and the relatively poor performance of the British private sector as compared to its international competitors.

4. *It is possible to transfer approaches employed in business management to the management of the NHS.* There are several features of the NHS which could be used to challenge this assumption. Most prominent among these are the power of the medical profession to define how health services are delivered, its cynical view of management, and the professional orientation to meet individual patient needs without reference to price or profit.

5. *The democratic nature of the NHS leads to poor management.* The Griffiths Report ignores the ideological foundations of the NHS in making this assumption. For example, the Report deems the process of consultation as 'labyrinthine' leading to 'institutionalized stagnation', it gives only the briefest references to CHCs and health authority members, it plays up the role of health authority chairs to the exclusion of other members of authorities and the recommendation that consultation procedures should be simplified and speeded up indicates health authorities were to be 'more managerial and less representative in character' (Day and Klein, 1983).

6. *The general manager can be the final decision-taker and manage the considerable power of professional groups in the NHS.* The Griffiths recommendations assume that general managers have the authority to curb the power of the medical profession and its strong ideas about the provision of services. The general manager's task is made more difficult by consultants' contracts remaining at regional level.

7. *Output measurement is straightforward in the NHS.* Outputs of the health service are varied. It provides employment to large numbers of people. It is the major producer of medical research and of training of nurses, doctors and many other occupations. However, the most essential of health service outputs are treatments and care provided to people. An important distinction has been drawn between outputs (the treatments provided to patients) and outcomes of care (the benefits to health). Existing literature on health outcomes, quality of life and client-satisfaction indicate the complexity of these issues.

8. *The NHS consists solely of hospital services.* The community and voluntary sectors are not explicitly discussed in the Griffiths Report. This begs the question: how can general managers be responsible for the total health care of the population when the hospital sector's links with these complex important sectors are not within the scope of their authority?

The discussion of the assumptions inherent in the Griffiths Report is not meant to convey political carping but merely to illustrate the points of debate that might have been taken up following the publication of the Report, yet rarely were these points debated in the commentary and furore which followed its publication. Rather the focus was almost exclusively on either the appointment of the new general manager, or the defence of a particular interest group. Furthermore, it is not surprising that some of these assumptions were made. A team of highly regarded and highly competent business people could not be expected to get to grips with the complexities of the NHS in the time available, particularly when there was so little available analysis of this complexity. Businessmen, like civil servants, academics, or any human being, carry their own ideological baggage which is bound to influence the way in which they view problems and makes it difficult to look at issues in a detached manner. Moreover, the Griffiths team did not have the luxury (as academics do) of saying they simply do not know the answer; as Sir Roy notes, the noise level in the NHS reached unprecedented heights at the time he and his team made his observations (Griffiths, 1991, p. 2). The Griffiths team had to come up with some analysis.

The Griffiths recommendations were supplemented with a number of managerially-driven changes. In 1983, the DHSS produced the first set of national NHS Performance Indicators (PIs) which enabled RHAs and DHAs to compare their performances on certain measures with national and regional norms and instructed English and Welsh health authorities to put cleaning, laundry and catering services out for tender. In 1984 annual reviews of units by DHAs were introduced, and in that year the DHSS required every DHA to include a cost-improvement programme within its short-term plan. In 1986, annual performance reviews of RHAs were to be undertaken by the NHS management board and these were to be, in addition to ministerial reviews, introduced in 1982. Finally, in 1987, Individual Performance Review (IPR) and Performance Related Pay (PRP) were introduced for general managers (see Pollitt, 1990, for a thorough review of these changes). All of these changes were introduced against a backdrop of increasingly tough financial constraints.

The Griffiths Report was subjected to critical examination by a number of writers. Day and Klein (1983), for example, suggested that the Report signified a change away from the mobilization of consent and towards the management of conflict, and they argued that if the health service was to move from a system based on the mobilization of consent to one based on the management of conflict – from one that had conceded to a variety of interest groups the right to veto change to one that gives managers the right to override objections – then that process would mean radical and painful change. Davies (1987) saw the Griffiths Report as an important part of a government strategy to gain a greater degree of centralized control and concluded that the Report indicated that centralization and the creation of a market in health care are not as opposed as they might at first seem. Petchey (1986) saw the report as transferring in an uncritical way managerial concepts from the private sector where he suggested management is less problematic than it is in the NHS, because in the former there exists consensus about both the ultimate objective of the organization (to make profits) and the criteria for evaluating alternative means of achieving that objective.

In addition to these analyses, a number of more empirically-based case studies have examined changes in the management of the NHS following the implementation of the Griffiths Report. I was part of a team whose own work was a study of this kind (Stewart *et al.*, 1988); funded by the then National Health Service Training Authority (NHSTA), the Templeton Study of DGMs primary aim was to produce training materials for district level general management. In selecting the sample the Templeton research team considered the recruitment figures of DGMs in September 1985 (see Table 4.2). The first five DGMs in the sample were selected from a management programme at Templeton College run by the research director and before the other members of the team were appointed. The other 15 DGMs were a stratified sample designed to give maximum coverage of background and type of district. The sample was deliberately biased to enable the study of DGMs from varied backgrounds. The eventual sample consisted of seven former NHS administrators, five non-NHS (three armed forces), two treasurers, two community physicians, two nurses and two hospital consultants.

The criteria for sampling included: professional background; the appointment date (the earliest appointment was September 1984, the latest June 1985); the region (there was at least one DGM from each region in England and one from Wales); teaching and non-teaching districts (four DGMs were from teaching districts); population (the district populations were relatively evenly spread from just over 100 000 to well over 500 000); budget, (revenue budgets ranged from under £20m to over £100m, with 15 receiving between £20m and £60m). The demographic characteristics of the districts were represented in almost the same proportion as the Office of Population, Censuses and Surveys (OPCS) clusters of demographic families of the country as a whole.

In the second year of the project there were opportunities for individual members of the research team to focus on particular issues associated with the development of general management, and to manage their own work whilst continuing to contribute to the original aims of the project. The material presented here draws on data collected for the project, however the following chapters represent a significantly different interpretation of the data generated as part of the Templeton study of DGMs (Stewart *et al.*, 1987–88; Stewart, 1989). The next chapter presents some of this material[2] and draws on figurational or process sociology and in particular Elias's notion of game models to help understand the priorities and actions of a sample of DGMs in their first four years as general managers following the implementation of the Griffiths Report.

5 DGMs' Priorities and Actions: An Eliasian Analysis

INTRODUCTION

A key assumption made by the Griffiths Report was that newly appointed general managers would be the catalyst for significant major change that would overcome some of the alleged weaknesses of the NHS as identified in the Report. This chapter explores the first four years of general management in 20 NHS districts, and, in doing so, explores empirically the assumptions made by the Griffiths team.

A striking finding of the chapter is the varying time and effort spent by the DGMs on what they perceived to be their key relationships. Most time was spent dealing with district management (either with district directors and unit managers as individuals, or with them as a district management board) and region (mainly the RGM), mostly because of the need to respond to Central initiatives and provide regional managers with information for monitoring purposes. The next most time-consuming relationship was with the chair, followed closely by DHA officials (mainly because of the need to feed the monthly DHA meeting agenda). Although doctors were considered a major management problem because of their ability to obstruct change, the time and effort spent directly working with doctors (as opposed to complaining about doctors) was far less than the time spent on managerial relationships. Managers, however, spent a great deal of time dealing with the financial consequences of the activity of doctors. Finally, significantly less time and effort was spent with nurses or with community groups. The chapter also draws on figurational or process sociology and in particular Elias's notion of game models to help understand the priorities and actions of the sample DGMs in their first four years as general managers.

WHAT DID DGMS DO?

A great deal of the Templeton sample DGMs' time was spent on what they saw as improving district management which involved clarifying the nature of the relationship between districts and units, coping with an array of demands from region and the Centre, and dealing with the DHA and the question of whom they were accountable to. This is not to imply that DGMs ignored questions of how health services were delivered or the appropriateness of health services, but merely to say that these were not what the majority of their time was directly focused on.

DGMs spent most of the first year in the job on designing structures and a new management board. Clarifying the relationships between members of the board and between districts and units continued to consume vast amounts of the DGMs' time. Members of the board struggled with understanding the scope of their role and their ability to influence the DGM and UGMs, and UGMs struggled with assessing their ability to influence the DGM and board members. This confusion was in part caused by the variation amongst DGMs across the country, in their basic assumptions on how to organize, lead and control the local health services, and about the parts general managers and others played in that process. Such diversity of views was not anticipated in the Griffiths Report. It is possible to present these differences in diagramatic forms as shown in Figure 5.1.

Model 1 illustrates the view held by some DGMs that the introduction of general management had fundamentally altered the balance of power in the NHS, away from district specialists to general managers. This group of DGMs often felt greatest affinity with UGMS – as one put it:

I have a common sense of direction with the UGMs, they are my people. I just don't seem to have that same sense of directional relationship with the district directors [Former district administrator].

One DGM argued that he and the UGMs were the core of management in his district and, to mark their elite status, another toasted his newly appointed UGMs with champagne.

Others in the sample inclined towards model 2. This group generally valued and sought to preserve the corporate influence of the district board and expected UGMs to act as its agent. As a former hospital consultant put it:

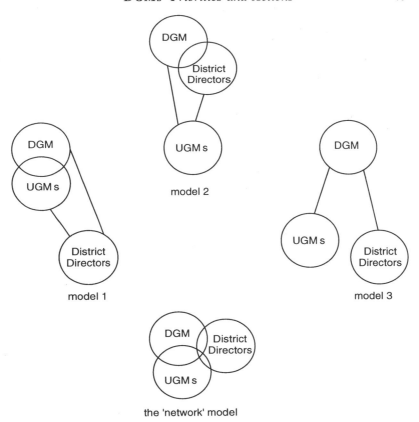

Figure 5.1 Models of relative status and influence

It is the district's job to provide direction and leadership: the UGMs are the chaps who do the actual work...

Those DGMs adopting model 3 had a sharper view of the DGM as the embodiment of district strategy in action. They stressed the virtues of structural clarity and quick and confident decision-making, clear differentation between roles and levels of management, and unambiguous targets and deadlines. One DGM (ex-army), for example, aimed to ensure that 'other people leave my office and they know what they have to do'. Another, a consultant, said:

The ideal situation is me sitting here and going out and visiting people occasionally, with nothing actually coming up from the unit that needs solving. I am going to institute a system of brownie points where managers will lose a point every time unit managers bring me a problem.

This group of DGMs were particularly critical of the previous experience of consensus management. Other DGMs accepted and even encouraged negotiation of objectives, and accountability within a team management structure (the network model).

Despite the amount of time spent by DGMs on district management issues, the question of which specialist management services were best located at unit level and which at district level, and why, was often not taken seriously. For example, the task of quality improvement was often given to a former DMT member (usually a nurse) with some 'slack' in their duties but without much regard to their qualifications, or the long-term implications for the delivery of health care.

The time DGMs spent on district management issues could be explained in a number of ways. For example, DGMs may have felt more comfortable in this area, or these relationship issues were more immediate and they may have felt these relationships had to be clarified before they could make wider changes, or they may have believed managerial relationships to be critical to improving health care.

THE PROBLEM OF REGIONS

Most DGMs argued that devolving power to units was hampered by the failure of regional managers to devolve power to the districts or to leave them alone to get on with managing local health services. For example:

I must say that DGMs are feeling more and more Centre-directed. Whatever happened to the idea that there was going to be more peripheral room for manoeuvre? Region like to say that they are doing just what the management board tells them, but they themselves do interfere in an excessive degree over such things as staff grading. It is not sensible that we should have to refer everything from grade 9 upwards to them.   (DGM)

There were a number of common criticisms made of regions. Firstly, regions were seen as over-bureaucratic:

The lingering bureaucracy at region and the DHSS may leave us fighting with one hand tied behind our backs.

I am irritated by region. On the one hand I am exalted because I am charismatic and imaginative, but I am held back by their petty restrictions on gradings of posts.

I am very worried that the district will become a postbox between region and units.

The increasing emphasis on bureaucracy was not matched by information about what priorities DGMs ought to be pursuing or any sensible statements about the strategic direction the NHS was to follow.

Some DGMs argued: 'the region seems to think it's only responsible for dishing out money and monitoring what the districts do'. Most felt 'unable to penetrate the treacle which permeates down all levels within the region' and were unsure if there was 'a lot of thinking going on behind closed doors or just no thinking at all'. There were concerns that what strategic planning there was was not linked to the district's own plans, and that districts were not involved in contributing to the formation of these plans:

We are all too remote, even allowing for the necessarily wider view at region . . . region should be using district's own drafts and forming the strategic plan.

The region's role in resource allocation invoked criticisms as one might expect in a period of financial constraints. These included not recognizing the operational effects of budget reductions, not listening to district managers so that policies were produced that districts could not afford to implement, and the exercise of favouritism, particularly towards teaching districts.

The region's role in relation to the Centre was often criticized. There were fears that region was not sufficiently conveying district views about the difficulties caused by the numerous national priorities. There were fears, too, that regions failed to challenge the Centre sufficiently and that region was not filtering out enough material from the DHSS. For example:

I find myself increasingly irritated by region, there is a continual constraint by very tight rules and procedures and their need for information which does not get used ... It is the opposite to what I see general management to be, it is a reflection of political require-ments.

It is a pity that the management board isn't protecting the Health Service from being a political football.

I am very worried that if general management doesn't work at the Centre, it will give a bad name at the periphery where it may well be working.

There were complaints from DGMs and other district managers both of over-monitoring and the impact this had on region's performance of their strategic role; for example:

It is really not clear why they [the region] need to come between us [the district] and the architects. And does region really need to have a say in where the light bulbs go?

We are jumping through hoops in order to demonstrate we can jump through hoops, without anyone pointing out that the hoops aren't actually achieving anything for the NHS.

Finally, regions were also criticized because of their continued holding of consultants' contracts.

If region are the employers of that group of consultants, then they ought bloody well to get their act together and not get us to flog away doing the foreman's job without having any authority to do it.

These criticisms need to be balanced by the references made by some DGMs to improvements at region and with the fact that many of the sample were not involved in regional work. As one DGM noted:

We can all throw hand-grenades over regional sandbags, but unless you are prepared to contribute, you can't complain ... You get the region and the Department that you deserve.

The largely negative attitudes to region, particularly those DGMs from within the NHS, appear to have been affected by changes which increased the power of regions to hold districts to account. These changes included: the development of the review process by which the Centre monitored progress on national priorities; the introduction of individual performance review and performance-related pay, with the 'grandparent' role at region giving the RGM a direct relationship with UGMs; and the development of information at region about district and unit performance, thus enhancing region's capacity and hence power to monitor.

RGMs interviewed put forward similar criticisms of the management board to those levelled at the region by the sample DGMs and other managers. For example:

Lack of Strategic Leadership

The management board is not proving to be a force in general management terms, they are piggy in the middle. [Reference to Ministers and the Department of Health] Unless the management style changes, this will always be the situation. That means being honest in parliament and accepting that they are a strategic authority and that the details that parliament sometimes required is [sic] not accessible to them.   [RGM]

My region is interventionist, and that is partly because the chair chooses to play it that way. It is also difficult to be any other way, given the impossibly crowded agenda that comes down from the Department ... It takes a few seconds for them to think of things up there, it takes us a few minutes to elaborate them, but when it hits the interface of clinicians, it is impossible.   [RGM]

One of the main problems with the Centre is that the agendas that come out of there are all about management process and not patient-care policies.   [RGM]

There are, in practice, very few Central initiatives, I can't think of one. I have had some very stern policy steers but no directives.
                                                             [RGM]

Too Much Bureaucracy

I sense that there aren't enough resources or skills to make this change happen. I feel that the pressure from the Centre has slackened off and all the old complacencies, all the old bureaucracy are anxious to rush round the door and come in again.   [RGM]

> I don't think the management board have developed a corporate role... They are two years behind everyone else and they are less general management oriented and have less of a corporate feel working in the department than is the case at region and districts. What you need is general management in the Department. The regional general managers call the management board 'Noah's Ark' because there are two of everything. [RGM]

In the view of this sample of DGMs and RGMs, as well as other managers and DHA members interviewed, the leadership from the Centre through the management board and regions promised by the Griffiths Report failed to materialize. Such leadership, Griffiths had argued, was pivitol to ensuring a successful general management process. There is no doubt that district management spent a great deal of time responding to requests from the Centre (communicated and elaborated by region). These requests often could be traced to a political debacle, the need to make a political point or justify existing policy or the need to cover a politician's 'gaffe'.

THE ACCOUNTABILITY QUESTION

The Griffiths Report was silent about the role of the DHA and public accountability more generally. Accountability was, however, an issue for DGMs in the second, third and fourth years of their job. Many DGMs spoke of the need to balance pressures from the management board and from region to whom they were managerially accountable, and from their chair and the DHA to whom they were publicly accountable:

> I feel torn in half between what is expected of me as an agent of the management board and the total needs for my region, particularly within a deprived region. [RGM]

> One of the biggest conflicts is with my regional chair who, after all, is a political appointment. He sees the region as an operating division HQ of the region and the district are the subsidiaries. I want a corporate view. [RGM]

Personalities proved to be important in resolving such issues. For example, the nature of the relationship between the district and regional chair could be an important influence on the relationship between RGM and DGM, and posed particular problems for DGMs who did not have a good relationship with their own chair. The influence of personalities is in part related to the uncertainty surrounding the relative roles and power of general management and public representatives following Griffiths.

An interesting finding of the research is the variation in the roles that district chairs played in their relationship with the DGM and in the time spent by chairs on their work for the NHS. Most chairs performed the roles described in the following two quotations:

> The chairman represents the authority. He interprets the authority's aims and wishes. He judges how it will react; he is the sounding board for the DGM. [DGM]

> The chairman is to make sure that all appropriate matters go before the authority to study; that a policy is arrived at which must be within the rules and regulations laid down. [DGM]

Some chairs saw themselves as merely waiting to hear when the DGM wanted them to become involved. Others saw themselves complementing the DGM's skills in a very cooperative relationship. A few thought the DGM's role was to manage the district and their role to take the flak. Many argued that chairs were the key interface between district and region and had the job of ensuring that regional managers understood the problems of the district.

DGMs also differed in their views of the importance of the DHA as a vehicle of public accountability and the time they should devote to it. The attitude amongst the sample towards the DHA could be described as ambivalent. This is well expressed by the following quotation:

> I don't feel driven by their views... I suppose we all play a game of 'we have got to get it through the DHA', and, whilst I value the opinions of some of the individual members, I am not sure that we really need collective views on any major decision facing us. But that worries me because it is not what I personally believe in. I think the DHA is an important institution, it is just that ours doesn't work that way. [DGM]

No DGM, however sceptical, dismissed the DHA. Those who failed to keep on good terms with members had considerable trouble rebuilding the relationship. There was also ambivalence about the time and effort DGMs and other managers spent in preparing for DHA meetings. Some found it an unwelcome burden while others, mostly former administrators, welcomed it because servicing the DHA was a useful source of influence, and the cycle of monthly meetings provided a useful discipline for keeping projects on target. At one extreme was a former administrator for whom the development of his DHA members was a top priority, at the other, another former administrator regarded the DHA as 'not being worth the time and effort'. In nearly all the districts there was a gap between what the DGM thought the DHA ought to be doing and how they judged it operated in practice. The range of roles played by DHA members, as reported by those DHA members and chairs interviewed, can be divided into four groups of activities:

1. Setting political/philosophical values.
2. Making decisions about policies and priorities.
3. Planned involvement in implementation or planning.
4. *Ad hoc* or one-off interventions.

DGMs argued that most activity of the DHA fell within category 4, whereas most members saw their performance equally in 2/3 and 4. Very few saw themselves in 1. Several DGMs spoke of the DHA's failure to tackle health care issues, preferring to concentrate on hotel service issues:

> I want them to stop thinking about dirty duvets and start thinking about how my district should develop a psychiatric service.

In short, DHAs were characterized by most of the sample as being interested in 'how things should be done, never what should be done' and 'lacking clear ideas of what they wanted DGMs to achieve'.

> They want to be led by the nose, and I don't want that from them, it is the uninformed leading the blind.

and some went so far as to say:

> There were times when their behaviour was a disgrace to major public service, consuming resources on this scale.[1]

DGMs gave three reasons for this situation. Firstly, some felt the DHA was not up to the job of making policy because of the poor quality of members:

I don't want members making policy if they are not equipped to do so. Their role is to challenge the policy put to them. I want to make them feel more positive, without raising their expectations too much as to their role. Their traditional refuge is to take up small causes.

Secondly, about half the sample believed DHAs ought to challenge government policy more and act as representatives of the local communities they served:

I am frustrated that the government line is followed so easily by DHA members.

One consequence of the perception of the ineffectiveness of the DHA was that most DGMs, even if believing strongly in the principle of public and open accountability, often secured decisions outside the formal DHA meeting.

A final reason given by DGMs for the ineffectiveness of the DHA was confusion surrounding the role of members following the Griffiths Report. DGMs (and often members) seemed unsure if they were there to check the details, shape the principles, or to be lay-managers themselves or the public watchdog of professional managers. In short, there seemed to be a lack of clarity amongst the sample and the chairs, about the appropriate mechanism of public accountability.

In many of the sample districts, a 'them' and 'us' situation existed with many DHA members disaffected. This view is supported by the findings of Christopher Ham (Ham, 1986). In the sample, rather than searching for a role, many of the DHA members were suffering from a massive erosion of morale. A major impact on the decline of morale was the pincer movement between the Centre (region or the DHSS) and the managers, which members believed was squeezing them out of the real role. Manpower targets, competitive tendering, accountability reviews, cost-improvement programmes, waiting-list initiatives, were all seen as testimony to this.

In observing the DHA meetings, the impression the research team had was that they resulted in very few policy shifts. But that did not necessarily mean that they were the rubber stamps they were sometimes accused of being. Many of the DGMs assessed what was likely to be acceptable to the DHA at an early stage of policy-making. It was always there in the background, as a conglomerate of local pressures that set strong limits around what managers could seek to change (Stewart *et al.*, 1987–88, No.3). The chair often played an important role as broker, allowing the DGM and members to assimilate and take account of each others' views. So – and in contrast to – many of the conclusions from academics examining the role of the DHA post-Griffiths Report, where the DHA has been seen as unimportant in influencing policy (Ham, 1986; Haywood, 1985), our data suggested that the DHA did have a significant role and did affect policy. So, whilst it might seem surprising that DGMs and their staff spent a great deal of time and effort on a body of little apparent influence, unclear roles and a host of problems, the reality is that the DHA, either informally or just by its very existence, did exert considerable influence on DGMs' actions and activities.

From the preceding discussion of the empirical findings relating to district management, regions and the accountability question, one begins to get a flavour of the complexity of the social relationships of which DGMs were a part. The effects of these relationships on the way in which DGMs pursued their job were immense. Regions, the Centre, DHAs and chairs, created an enormous amount of paperwork for the DGM and his or her team, either in the name of public accountability or because of the need to respond to the consequences of the interactions between government, DHSS and region. The power struggles between the UGMs, district directors and DGMs also were time-consuming if the DGM was at all sensitive to such issues.

THE 'PROBLEM OF DOCTORS'

Not surprisingly, the power of doctors was the issue the sample talked about most in the second, third and fourth years of the job. All of the sample faced the difficult task of getting doctors to accept the management view that their clinical freedom should be counterbalanced by an awareness of, and responsibility for, the effective management of resources. Their task was made more difficult by various problems and uncertainties. Firstly, they often did not know the exact nature of the doctors' contractual obligations because contracts were with the region. Secondly, the majority lacked relevant clinical knowledge and were often hesitant to discuss professional and technical standards and indeed felt vulnerable in such discussions with doctors. Thirdly, there were few incentives available to encourage doctors to become more involved in management outside their group or department. A management post took doctors away from a well-trodden and well-rewarded career path. Some of the medical representatives in the sample districts referred to the price of their involvement in management in terms of increased work-load, financial loss and tensions with other colleagues.

A few quotations illustrate the difficulty the sample DGMs found in implementing the Griffiths recommendation to involve doctors more closely in management:

> The doctors lead the technology, and therefore the pattern of service. Unless managers get the doctors with them, everything else is just window-dressing. That's where you have got to get change ... there never will be a better time.

> The success or failure of optimizing health care ultimately depends on doctors.

> The glorious Griffiths image of the DGM cutting through the bureaucratic undergrowth is just hogwash. You can cut through it as much as you like, but when you have done it, you are just left there against the consultants who are saying 'no'.

> The consultants are a devoted bunch, but I bet no-one warned the outsider DGMs how little control they would have over this major resource.

THE 'PROBLEM OF MANAGERS': THE DOCTORS' VIEW

If doctors were 'a problem' for managers, it is equally true that, from the perspective of doctors, it was managers who were 'the problem'. DGMs were often not aware of how suspicious and fearful the consultant body was of general management. In particular, those doctors I interviewed feared that general managers would try to encroach on their professional independence, their freedom to determine their working patterns, even their clinical freedom. They also feared that managers would remove them from the decision-making machinery, leaving the managers free to ignore medical advice. A related fear was that general management would entail an erosion of what doctors considered to be 'special' NHS values. 'Thank God we didn't get someone from Sainsbury's', said one medical informant, giving voice to many in the Health Service who assert that there is something special and different about health that is not amenable to a managerial or commercial approach. Again, while there is undoubtedly some validity in this argument, it is also overlain with strong ideological overtones which are called into play in conflict situations of this kind.

Most medical informants felt that discussions of resources were somehow improper, and believed such discussions conflicted with their responsibility to the individual patient. There was a related fear that general management may lead to a finance-led view of health care which would force doctors to make decisions on economic rather than clinical grounds. One group of consultants in response to a budget deficiency invoked the Hippocratic Oath, refusing to have anything to do with decisions about priorities.

Doctors were also afraid that their autonomy would be curtailed. They often suspected managers of being appointed as bureaucratic henchmen, put in post to carry out dictates from the Centre.[2] Doctors tend to have a poor grasp of, and little respect for, managerial skills or structures. For example:

> The unit general managers are just too junior to be accepted by us as a group. We prefer to relate to the chair.

They also believed general managers were out of touch with what actually goes on in the NHS:

> It is the doctors who know the problems and who are patient oriented. Administrators[3] do not have the background, so will never be able to relate properly to us. They need us, we don't need them. (Consultant from a sample district)

Some believed:

> Most doctors are more intelligent than DGMs and they tend to know it. (Consultant from a sample district)

Doctor interviewees often found managerial phrases uncomfortable to use and generally distasteful. For example one consultant argued:

> I hate the word 'customer', it conjures up images of baked beans on a shelf.

A few doctor interviewees admitted (confidentially) that they had no idea what some of the managerial jargon meant and found themselves arguing with managers in order to cover up their ignorance. Sometimes medical informants admitted that they misunderstood the role of advice and negotiation and were ineffective in the medical advisory machinery. In one district, for example, they expected to appoint the acute unit general manager by a consultants' ballot. Doctors often stated quite clearly that, in their view, managers were there to oil the wheels and ensure adequate facilities and equipment as they were needed. When it came to influencing policy they preferred to deal with the district chair, believing him or her to have power. They had no clear idea as to what regions or the management board did. Some had never heard of the management board, let alone the Griffiths Report.

NON-PROBLEMATIC RELATIONSHIPS

There were a number of relationships that DGMs found non-problematic in the sense that these groups did not take up a great deal of the DGMs' time, and were not troublesome. They were often dealt with in terms of being one of the many groups the DGM had to send consultation documents to.

There were very few spontaneous comments from the sample on nursing or, indeed, other para-medical professions. Rarely did nursing figure in any of the policy discussions I observed. Most of the interview comments on nursing centred on difficulties the DGMs had in finding a role for the former district nursing officer, most of whom went into the quality assurance posts.

A number of local interest groups were referred to over the period of the study without DGMs reporting them to significantly influence their activities. In general DGMs, whatever their background, did not want to ride rough-shod over the CHCs and acknowledged them as 'the voice of the community', but in practice they deemed them ineffective, suffering from a bureaucratic committee structure and warring factions and described the CHC as 'tame', 'passive', 'tedious', 'a complaint-collecting organization' and 'political'. Very little time was spent on this relationship, indeed only two DGMs – both former administrators – regularly attended the CHC's meetings. CHCs were on the mailing list for consultation documents, but were never considered by the sample as a body that had to be actively influenced to get policies agreed.

Similarly, little comment was made about the role of the local authority. Most districts seemed to be building bridges, but usually this was through the DGM and director of social services meeting on a regular basis, mainly to exchange information rather than negotiate policy. The overall conclusion that one can draw from the data on this relationship is that there was great confusion about the relative responsibilities of the health authority and the local authority.

The trade unions were another local group occasionally mentioned. Most DGMs delegated industrial relations matters to either the personnel manager or to the units, with DGMs being a last resort. Some DGMs were more active in courting their local MPs than others, although MPs were regarded by all DGMs as important people to keep informed of local issues relating to health. Only two DGMs mentioned forging relationships with the private health sector. GPs were rarely mentioned, except in the context of the district board where there was a representative, although some DGMs had made efforts to meet with the chair of the family practitioner committee. Voluntary groups and patient groups were also very rarely mentioned, but some DGMs did attend various meetings and gave talks to community bodies.

DGMs from outside the NHS were surprised at the number of diverse interests associated with health care and seemed to make more overtures to local community groups than those previously working within the health service. The attitude of more-seasoned NHS managers was to keep an eye on local groups and make sure they didn't do any harm. Most of the sample claimed (when asked) that they cared about community views, but were very cynical about the mechanisms available to represent them.

Several DGMs made efforts to inform the public of what was happening within the NHS, either through press briefings (the usual stimulation for this was a financial crisis) and the production of annual reports. One district appointed a public relations manager to 'put money in the bank with the community in times of crises'. Only one DGM mentioned the role of the health service as employer and was active in careers activities within schools. Occasionally in the interviews, or during observation periods, there were comments made about the importance of the public driving the direction of the health service rather than professionals, but given the lack of effort put into debating this issue, this concern could be seen as lip-service.

It seems from the data that local groups, nurses, paraprofessions, GPs and trade unions were not important relationships to DGMs in the sense of influencing their management activity. They were relatively powerless within the figuration of relationships which involved DGMs, and were monitored relationships rather than influential relationships. Furthermore, despite the Griffiths Report's emphasis on the importance of the consumers of health care, very little attention was paid to consumer representatives or consumers as people whom the service should involve in decisions about what health services should be providing. Rather, most DGMs sought to deal with the 'consumer issue' as defined by Griffiths by making efforts to improve the quality of health care as defined by general management. This is discussed in the next section.

IMPROVING QUALITY

The Griffiths Report placed great emphasis on improving quality. General management was thought by the Griffiths team to be capable of facilitating improvements in service delivery and it was thought possible to measure such improvements. Most DGMs, however, were cynical as to whether quality improvement or quality assurance really represented new concepts, or were merely labels for what was happening already. The general feeling amongst the sample was that whilst there had been no explicit policy on quality before Griffiths, improving the quality of health care had been a central objective of consensus management. DGMs with experience of the NHS said there had been a 'complacent', rather than a 'negative' attitude towards quality; of 'quality being partly around, but no-one positively asking what the quality of the service was like'; 'of targets being in numbers and finance but not in quality'; 'of an assumption that someone else is dealing with the standards of care, but that quality is provided'. Newcomers to the service, although sharing some of the concerns about a complacent attitude to quality, were impressed by the degree of commitment amongst NHS staff to give a good service in very difficult circumstances and with inadequate resources.

Certainly in the months following the government's acceptance of the Griffiths recommendations, quality had become a catch-phrase and there was an increase in activity explicitly in this area. DGMs in the sample attributed this partly to the emphasis placed on the importance of the consumer in the Griffiths Report, but also recognized other factors. These included:

- the general consumer movement which impacted on many service industries in the United Kingdom;
- the need for professions, particularly doctors, to take a more active part in management, which required managers to become involved in issues of professional and technical standards;
- the government's priority care areas, for example, mental health and geriatrics, which demanded a rethink of what services should be available and how they should be provided;
- and the government's demand to ensure value for money and to measure performance against effectiveness.

However, there were varying views amongst sample members as to what quality improvement involved and these views often reflected the previous professional background. For the former administrators, quality was commented upon as an inescapable part of the job or as a way of 'curbing the egocentricity of disciplines', or 'a way of testing if doctors are doing their job.'

The former consultants and nurses in the sample saw quality as 'everyone's business'. This group of DGMs did not believe that one individual could be responsible for quality, rather:

> Quality must be an attitude of mind which permeates the organization, it must be a part of everyone's job and everybody's performance must be judged by the extent to which they have contributed to improving the quality of the service.

Those DGMs new to the NHS had a significantly different view of what quality as an issue involved. For five of the six, quality involved inspection, 'a dirty word in the NHS'. A former industrialist argued that his ultimate aim was to 'put ourselves out of business. I want people to lead happy, helpful lives and to keep out of doctors' clutches.' Another former industrialist simply felt that 'Quality has to take a backseat to the need to keep things going.'

Former community physicians saw quality as democratizing care and 'asking what real health needs are' and former treasurers consistently raised the theme that quality was inextricably linked with ensuring value for money:

> The general manager's role has to be to make the most effective and efficient use of resources available, but also make a judgement

about the right balance between providing the quantity of service to patients and wishes of others to provide quality.

The overriding characteristic of these different views is vagueness. When pushed, DGMs were incapable of spelling out what the phrases, that tripped so elegantly and automatically off their tongues actually meant. In the face of this uncertainty DGMs appear to have relied on their past experience.

About half the sample did not routinely mention 'quality' in the interviews despite setting in motion a number of changes in the organization and delivery of health care. Some former DAs and health professionals were very cynical and questioned whether the recent emphasis on quality improvement was merely a way of diffusing the debate on the lack of money in the health service. One manager argued that staff working in chronically bad working conditions who had not got the money or tools to do a good job, would think it 'hot air' and resent being asked to improve the quality of the service they provide, given the obstacles with which they had to contend.

About a quarter of the sample, despite being strong on rhetoric, sparked few if any quality improvement initiatives, claiming that quality improvement had taken a back seat to keeping things going and responding to external pressures from the department, region and the chair. One former industrialist deliberately marked time until he knew what quality initiatives had produced results in other districts.

From the data collected from the districts, quality initiatives spanned four broad areas: consumerism, professional and technical standards, establishing an appropriate balance of services in line with national priorities and ensuring value for money. Most effort which was overtly recognized as being in quality improvement was in the area of consumerism. Hotel services like reception, laundry and catering were reviewed. 'Shop window' jobs were examined to ensure that staff were attentive to patients. Many districts sought to improve the style of care and held staff communication training courses. Quality circles and quality suggestions schemes were introduced in order to tap staff ideas. Complaints procedures were often reviewed and some districts used patient satisfaction surveys to assess whether the customer was receiving an acceptable service. Improving patient information was also made a priority in most districts. In justifying the emphasis on hotel services, comparisons were often made to private health care. As a former nurse put it:

It is the task of general management to make the organization everywhere appear to be providing a service and to be welcoming people. That happens in private health care. To some extent that is because they have the money, but some of it is the organization saying it is important to do that.

There was significantly less effort put into improving professional and technical standards. While some DGMs spent time with clinical professions and sought to put across the message that 'better doctoring and nursing consider questions of quality', for most, and for reasons outlined earlier, it was simply a no-go area.

Most DGMs considered quality issues and the balance of health services and talked about this under planning and the poor guidance on priorities given by those at the Centre. A dilemma for all of them was at what point do managers say that they cannot improve quality, but must change the quantity. 'When do we say we have to live with the current quality to have quantity?' Value for money and the link to quality was mainly talked about in relation to living within existing and, in the sample's view, inadequate budgets.

The emphasis DGMs placed on consumerism and the hotel aspects of health care may be explained in a number of ways. Firstly, it was an area where the DGM could take a lead and make a tangible contribution to improving quality without having to engage in battles with doctors. Secondly, DGMs found it easier to apply the Griffiths agenda to hotel services, for, by making improvements in this area, they were visibly doing something for consumers. Thirdly, DGMs were diffident in entering the clinical profession's domain because of the powerful medical arguments doctors could marshall. Improving medical care was sidestepped and became part of the largely nascent desire to include doctors in management. Fourthly, most DGMs lacked tools (that made sense to them) with which to measure quality and quality improvements. Some claimed that they needed help from community physicians which, for one reason or another, they were not getting. Finally, one former industrialist saw the hotel and consumer side of quality as a means by which he could influence clinical outcomes. He believed an alliance with consumers would enable him to exert public pressure on professions to think more carefully about their service.

The Templeton research indicated that there were several unplanned and unanticipated outcomes of the implementation of the Griffiths proposals; indeed, in some cases these outcomes were the very reverse of the objectives set out in the Griffiths Report. The major findings can be summarized as follows:

1. There appears to have been a trend towards greater centralization of power within the health service, accompanied by increased bureaucracy, a proliferation of policy objectives and a shrinkage of resources, all of which served to curtail the freedom of those working at the district level to meet the health care needs of the local population.

2. There appears to have been more, rather than less, confusion in terms of accountability structures in the NHS. At the time they were appointed, the general managers in our study were extremely clear that they were accountable to their District Health Authority and, through it, to the local community. However, our data suggested that in the everyday practice of their job, the actions of District General Managers were constrained, in particular, by three overlapping chains of accountability comprising: (i) the Secretary of State, and the chairs of the Regional and District Health Authorities; (ii) the DHSS, the Regional Health Authority and the District Health Authority; and (iii) the Management Board and the Regional General Manager (RGM). These constraints had the effect of obscuring what the general managers originally perceived as their accountability to the public and also led them to play down, in relative terms, the involvement of nurses, trades unions and other local groups in the formation and implementation of policy.

3. At the district level, general managers had radically divergent views of both their own leadership role and of the place of professional and, in particular, medical advice in the implementation of their agenda for change. There was also a significant relationship between general managers' views of how they should act in what was a new role within the NHS and their previous occupational experiences, with many managers drawing upon their previous experiences as a basis for structuring their new role.

4. The status and power of the nursing profession appears to have declined within the new managerial structure. Nurses were often given quality assurance roles which were frequently seen as 'non-jobs' and this was associated with reduced influence in shaping policy decisions.

5. Because general management was introduced at a time when the government, led by Margaret Thatcher, was seeking dramatically

to reduce public expenditure, the introduction of general management became inextricably linked with the idea of cuts in public expenditure and, as a consequence, notions of improving the management process were often viewed cynically.

6. Doctors, as an established and powerful group within the NHS, remained largely sceptical about the introduction of general management and frequently saw it as part of a government strategy designed to undermine, if not the NHS itself, then certainly the conception of the NHS held by many doctors. They did not flock to take up general management posts as the government had hoped and were deeply suspicious of general management as a vehicle to improve health services. They did not see themselves as 'natural managers' as Griffiths believed would be the case.

7. Improvements in quality mainly took the form of improvements in 'hotel services' rather than in the quality of medical care. In part this was because improvements in the former did not involve managers in challenging the power of clinicians, and, in part, it was because they were easier to measure and could be taken as an indication of managerial 'success'.

Most of these findings are consistent with those of other researchers who have examined the impact of the changes introduced following the Griffiths Report. For example, a project which was concerned with the evaluation of general management and which was carried out by the Trade Union Research Unit in 1987, found a management structure which was in many ways marked by confusion rather than clarity of managerial responsibility. Robinson, Strong and Elkan (1989) found that the new decision-making structure had resulted in the wholesale abolition of the established nursing hierarchy and that nurses were now in a 'hotch-potch' of jobs. Strong and Robinson (1990) found that 'doctors still gave orders' and that nursing had relatively little managerial importance. Kingston and Rowbottom (1989) described a situation characterized by confused roles, unworkable responsibilities, inadequate arrangements for accountability, proliferating committees and clumsy procedures.

This brief and, admittedly, selective overview of the consequences of the implementation of the Griffiths Report is not intended to be comprehensive. Neither is it intended to suggest that the implementation of the Griffiths Report should, in some simplistic way, be deemed a failure. In this context it is relevant to point out that several studies concluded that decision-making following the introduction of general management had speeded up, though it is perhaps important to treat this finding with some caution since it is a finding about people's perceptions of decision-making, not about decision-making as such. For example Harrison *et al.* found that managers in the areas of finance, personnel, planning and nursing were likely to believe that decision-making had speeded up, especially if they had previously worked at the regional level, whereas clinicians generally saw the district management team as having merely changed its name and reported no significant change in decision-making (Harrison, Hunter, Marnoch and Pollitt, 1992). However, it is not the intention here either to provide a comprehensive summary of the consequences of the implementation of the Griffiths Report, or to offer a general evaluation of the effectiveness of general management. The point is a more simple one, but one which raises an interesting problem in relation to how we can best analyse processes of managed social change. The central issue is that all the research on general management, including that in which I was involved, indicates that the implementation of general management did not work out in the way in which either Sir Roy Griffiths and his team or the Government had intended; there were, that is to say, a number of unanticipated consequences of the introduction of general management and, at least in some cases, those consequences were not only unexpected but were actually the very reverse of what had been intended and hoped for by those responsible for initiating these changes.

The question which immediately arises, therefore, is how we can account for what all studies have identified as a significant gap between the intentions and aspirations expressed in the Griffiths Report and what the introduction of general management was able to deliver. Many of the empirical studies of general management have failed to pose this question, let alone provided an adequate answer. This may in part be a consequence of the funding arrangements for these studies and the interests of the funding bodies. It may also reflect the absence of helpful concepts or frameworks because of the general lack of interest of medical sociologists in health care management (Cox, 1991), and the feeling amongst many academics working in the area of management studies that the health service is not a fruitful research and consultancy area, though this latter perception is now beginning to change particularly since the introduction of the internal market in the NHS following the 1989 White Paper. Some of the studies of general management do, however, offer explanations for the gap between the objectives expressed in the Griffiths Report and what general management was able to deliver and, before offering a framework for understanding such discrepancies, it may be useful to examine some of these alternative explanations.

Strong and Robinson, reporting on the implementation of the Griffiths Report in a sample of districts, concluded that the reason for the failure of general management to meet expectations was that, although the Griffiths model was a radical one, it was implemented within an institution which had a very different tradition of central planning. They argue that, as a consequence, the changes following the Griffiths Report represented only a partial break with the past and that general management was, as they put it, 'trapped inside the old NHS hierarchy' with what they describe as continuing 'political interference'. They concluded that:

> whereas writers such as Drucker had urged 'socialist competition' for this special type of service institution, the NHS remained monolith. Griffiths might have installed a line of command and imposed a micro-management ethos but it had left its macro-structure intact.
> (Strong and Robinson, 1990, p. 183)

Sir Roy Griffiths himself hinted at the problems associated with such a compromise in a public lecture in 1991. He indicated that change had not occurred as fast as he would have liked and suggested that this had been largely because of poor leadership from the Supervisory Board and the Management Board. Both, he argued, 'were absolutely correct in concept' but were 'half-hearted in their implementation'. Major policy issues, he suggested, were left uncovered; there was no proper attempt to establish objectives for the Health Service as a whole and no concentration on outcomes (Griffiths, 1991, p. 12).

In addition, Strong and Robinson argued that local processes also affected the transition between the old and the new styles of management. In particular, they point to the way that previous structures had sometimes foreshadowed the new regime, to the fact that the old district management team still existed and moulded events, and to the influence of the new District General Managers' differing backgrounds and preferred styles of working. These points are unfortunately not elaborated.

McNulty (1989) found that conflict between clinicians and managers – conflict which was associated with the very different cultural assumptions held by these groups – substantially reduced managerial effectiveness and made it difficult for managers to achieve the changes which they desired. Harrison, Hunter, Marnoch and Pollitt explained the gap between what the Griffiths Report promised and what general management was able to deliver in terms of tensions or problems internal to the Griffiths model. They highlighted in particular three key problems. Firstly, they argued that the managerialism of the Griffiths model was founded on distrust and that this contrasted radically with the consensus mode of working, associated with the 1974 and 1982 reorganizations of the NHS, which rested on trust. They wrote:

> to transform such a system into one in which identifiable individuals have to take personal responsibility for quantified targets, is to shine a strong, harsh light into processes of intricate political bargaining which may require degrees of flexibility, creative ambiguity and even downright secrecy in order to function most efficiently. This may be no bad thing, but it does cast doubt on the claim that Griffiths made to be able to preserve the good features (unidentified) of the consensus management system alongside the new model.   (Harrison *et al.*, 1992, p. 68)

A second problem identified by Harrison *et al.* was the failure of the Griffiths Report to offer a convincing analysis of the relationship between the business of running the NHS and the workings of the political system within which the service is set:

> The NHS is a major, and highly popular public institution. It generates the never-ending stream of issues of local or national political interest. Underpaid 'angels' (nurses or ambulance staff); new wonder treatments; lengthening waiting lists; doctors with controversial diagnostic approaches to children who are suspected of having been sexually abused, other children who are kept waiting for treatment for life-threatening conditions because of staff shortages; scandalous conditions in long-stay geriatric or mental hospitals – the list is endless. Ministers have seldom been able to resist the pressures to intervene when one of these issues flares up, and there is no obvious reason to expect they will exert greater self-restraint in the future.   (Harrison *et al.*, 1992, p. 69)

Finally, Harrison *et al.* argued that the revolution in managerial culture proposed by Griffiths was posited on the development of tolerably clear objectives, which simply did not emerge. They concluded that:

the implementation of the Griffiths model has been handicapped by tensions and limitations which were inherent in the original report, by flawed understanding of the management problems of the NHS and by wider developments (the failure of government to set clear priorities, plus the deteriorating financial situation) which were beyond its remit.   (Harrison *et al.*, 1992, p. 72)

Harrison *et al.* develop a theoretical perspective drawn from political science in which concepts of power, organizational culture and puzzlement or uncertainty are to the fore in explaining the relationships between doctors and managers, and the problems general managers faced in implementing general management policies within the NHS. The first chapter of their book is devoted to an explanation of these key concepts, but the book is perhaps a little disappointing in the sense that there is no overt attempt to apply these concepts to their data on general management. For example, in summarizing the reasons for what might be called the 'implementation gap' Harrison *et al.* do not draw explicitly on the three explanatory concepts they set out earlier in their book. Rather, they state that:

implementation failure is not necessarily the fault of general management. Indeed, in some of our districts, general managers struggled against all the odds to make progress. The fact they either failed or were only partially successful has less to do with general management *per se* than with the prevailing culture, resource context, organisational relationships (both intra- and inter-), uncertainties in the external environment and the power dependencies among key groups or stake-holders. They conspired to act as a more powerful determinant of policy implementation than general management. Where successful progress was possible in particular local circumstances, the converse prevailed though instances of this were, given the complexities, understandably more rare.
                                  (Harrison *et al.*, 1992, p. 112)

Many of these studies shed helpful light on the 'implementation gap', and the work presented earlier in this chapter confirmed the importance of several processes identified in other studies. For example, the sample of general managers identified the difficulty of dealing with doctors – the 'problem of doctors' as the managers saw it – as perhaps the greatest single difficulty with which they had to cope, though it should be noted that interviews with clinicians also indicated that what from the point of view of managers was the 'problem of doctors' was, from the point of view of doctors, the 'problem of managers'. The data confirms that there were major problems in the relatively uncritical transfer to a politically sensitive public service such as the NHS of managerial concepts and strategies which had been developed in the rather different context of private industry. However, while many of these studies provide, to a greater or lesser degree, useful analyses of the 'implementation gap' within a particular organization during a particular period of time, it could be argued that none of them provides a model which offers an adequate understanding, on a more theoretical level, of the processes involved. I would further argue that such a general model *is* required, for without a continual interdependence – Elias (1987, p. 20) referred to 'an uninterrupted two-way traffic' – between the development of detailed knowledge and synthesizing models, the empirical and the theoretical, the collection of detailed knowledge of particular situations will be of limited use; for it is only by the use of synthesizing models that we can generalize from one situation to another, and only by means of constant checking against empirical results can we test the adequacy of our synthesizing models.

Underlying not only the Griffiths Report but also the work of many writers who have analysed the implementation of that report, is an implicit assumption that with 'proper' information and 'sound' management it is possible to implement change in such a way that the outcome, within relatively closely defined limits, will be more or less what was intended. The Griffiths Committee, for example, clearly imagined that it was possible to implement the recommendations in such a way that the desired outcome would be achieved and when this desired outcome was not achieved, the implementation gap was attributed largely to what might be termed failures or errors, for example poor leadership, half-hearted implementation and the absence of a 'proper' attempt to establish objectives for the health service as a whole. In contrast to Griffiths' own explanation (1991), which rather suggests that if everyone had tried harder and done their job properly then the implementation would have been much more of a success, a number of other analyses, and particularly the sociologically more satisfactory ones, have focused upon social rather than individual processes, some of which involve socially structured tensions or conflicts which have impeded a fuller and more effective implementation of the Griffiths proposals (Cox, 1991; Strong and Robinson, 1990; Harrison *et al.*, 1992; Pettigrew, Ferlie and McKee, 1992).

However, even these rather more satisfactory analyses do not adequately theorize the unintended outcomes of the policy implementation process and, in particular, none of these approaches offers a general explanatory model, which suggests that such an implementation gap should be regarded as the norm rather than as something unexpected. It is precisely in order to theorize more adequately this aspect of managed change that the work of Norbert Elias (outlined in Chapter 3), and in particular his game models, is useful.

Elias (1978, p. 73) sees game models as a means of isolating in close focus the intertwining of the aims and actions of pluralities of people, thereby making these complex processes of interweaving more easily understandable. On a theoretical level the game models, like Elias's more general process-sociological approach of which they are a part, are designed as a way of helping to move towards a resolution of the age-old problem within sociology which has variously been described as the relationship between the individual and society, free will and determinism, personality and social structure or, in its currently popular formulation, the agency/structure debate. In this regard, Elias's approach recognizes that human action is, to a greater or lesser degree, consciously directed towards achieving certain goals and that all human action necessarily involves both cognition and emotion, and in this sense it fully takes into account the fact that humans are thinking and feeling beings, and that in a highly individualized society such as modern Britain we each have our own more or less individual pattern of intentions, preferences and desires. At the same time, however, Elias also emphasizes that the outcomes of complex social processes cannot be explained simply in terms of the intentions of individuals; indeed, it is important to recognize that the *normal* result of complex processes involving the interweaving of the more or less goal-directed actions of large numbers of people includes outcomes which no-one has chosen and no-one has designed. Social processes of this kind, involving outcomes which were unplanned and unforeseen, were termed by Elias (1987, p. 99) 'blind social processes'. It may be useful to say a little more about this concept of Elias, and the relationship between blind and planned processes of change.

BLIND SOCIAL PROCESSES AND THE PLANNING PROCESS

Elias has pointed out that it is possible to identify a number of long-term social processes which were unplanned but which involved change in a particular direction. A good example is provided by Elias's own work (1978, 1982) on civilizing processes, but there are numerous other examples which one could cite. One of the most obvious is the long-term trend towards the increasing differentiation of social functions. The aspect of this process which has been most studied by social scientists is probably that involving the increasing division of labour, a trend which can be verified relatively easily, for example, by comparing the number of occupational groups designated by a special term in societies at different stages of social development. However, it should be noted that the trend towards a growing differentiation of social functions does not simply involve a growing division of labour, but is much more all-embracing and can be observed not only in the production of goods but in the administration of states, in science and technology and in almost all areas of social life. As further examples of long-term unplanned processes one might mention the lengthening of chains of interdependency – a process which Elias analysed in some detail in *The Civilizing Process* and which involves a greater number of people, over greater geographical areas, becoming increasingly interdependent – or, perhaps rather more familiar to most people, processes involving the routinization or secularization of many aspects of social life.

What, then, for those involved in managing change, is the relevance of an understanding of longer-term, unplanned processes? In this context it is important to remind ourselves that, as Elias (1977, pp. 138–9) has noted, the steady growth of more conscious and deliberate attempts to manage processes of change through the growth of institutionalized forms of social planning is a development which is characteristic of a specific phase of a broader *unplanned* development. Yet those involved in designing and implementing processes of managed social change hardly ever bother to ask questions about the long-term, unplanned structural changes in human societies which have provided the basis, particularly in the twentieth century, for the rapid growth of precisely those kinds of planning projects in which they are themselves involved.

To a considerable degree, this failure to recognize the long-term interweaving of planned and unplanned processes is a consequence of the fact that those involved in planning are all too often involved in networks of relationships which constrain them to deliver results in the short term. Almost all research concerned with the management of change – and this is perhaps particularly true of recent research concerned with managing change within the NHS – is very much concerned with the here and now. This present-orientation – Elias (1987) called it the 'retreat into the present' – is often justified in terms of a dichotomy which emphasizes the practical rather than the theoretical, with the implication that such a 'practical', present-centred orientation provides a better guide to planning. It is however difficult to see any reasonable basis on which such a claim could be sustained and, indeed, it is perhaps particularly when considering the practical relevance of sociological studies that one sees most clearly the limited value of a sociology which is concerned exclusively with the here and now. Underpinning such present-centred research, as Elias noted, is an almost complete lack of awareness of the long-term unplanned developments which have created the conditions that have made possible a greater degree of deliberate planning and *within which all planned projects take place.*

There are clearly considerable risks involved in social planning which is based exclusively on present-centred, here-and-now investigations. Elias (1977, p. 138) pointed out, for example, that it is only through striving to understand long-term processes that we can move towards obtaining an orientation that is sufficiently wide-ranging and reality-congruent to enable us to decide whether short-term practical measures designed to overcome difficulties and disadvantages will not, in the longer term, produce difficulties and disadvantages that are even greater. A fuller understanding of the way in which the actions of interdependent people interweave to produce trends which no one has planned or intended, and which then constitute and constrain the perceptions, goals and actions of people, can only be adequately understood if we take a longer-term developmental perspective. As another process-sociologist, Johan Goudsblom, has nicely put it, 'in the development of human societies, yesterday's unintended social consequences are today's unintended social conditions of "intentional human actions"' (Goudsblom, 1977, p. 149).

It might be objected that Elias's concept of blind or unplanned social processes involves nothing more than what has long been recognized by social scientists under another name. In this respect it is true that the idea of unintended or unanticipated consequences of social action has a long history and that it may be found in the work of some classical sociologists and philosophers, while in economics it may be found – though in a specific and very limited way – in the work of free market advocates such as Hayek (1945). Within sociology, the idea of unanticipated consequences is probably most closely associated with the work of Robert Merton (1936, 1949).

However, as Mennell (1989) has pointed out, there are some important differences between the concept of unanticipated consequences, as developed by Merton, and Elias's concept of blind social processes. Mennell points out that Merton focuses, in particular, on what may be regarded as an oddity of social life, namely the 'self-fulfilling' prophesy, with passing mention of the converse 'self-contradicting' prophesy. Such situations may have a certain fascination but they are, suggests Mennell, fundamentally a trivial diversion, because they are simply an unusual and rather special case of something which is not only much more common, but also of considerably greater theoretical significance. Mennell (1989, p. 258) expresses what he sees as the major difference between Merton and Elias thus:

> Much more clearly than Merton, Norbert Elias recognizes that people's knowledge of the figurations in which they are caught up is virtually always imperfect, incomplete and inaccurate. The strategies of action which they base on this inadequate knowledge therefore more often than not have consequences which they do not foresee. So unanticipated consequences are not a curious footnote to sociology but nearly universal in social life. For Merton, the self-fulfilling prophecy is like a boomerang: the consequences of men's [sic] actions rebound upon their initiators. For Elias, the analogy is much less exotic and much more commonplace: like the effect of a stone dropped into a pool, the consequences of people's actions ripple outwards through society until they are lost from sight. Their effects are felt, not at random but according to the structure of the figuration in which they are enmeshed, by people who may well be quite unknown to each other and unaware of their mutual interdependence.

There is another, and perhaps more fundamental, difference between Elias's work and that of Merton. Whereas Merton's discussion of unintended consequences was largely individualistic, Elias's focus was on pluralities of people, for Elias was concerned not with single acts but with aggregates of intentional acts. The largely individualistic character of Merton's position was explicitly recognized by Merton himself in his early classic article which, he acknowledged, dealt mainly 'with isolated purposive acts rather than with their integration into a coherent system of action' (1936, p. 895). Though Merton's later (1949) discussion is perhaps less individualistic, it remains the case that Elias's approach focuses far more systematically, not on isolated individual acts, but on the complex interweaving of the actions of many people, not all of whom will even be known to each other.

At this stage it may be useful to turn to a more detailed examination of Elias's game models in order to see, in particular, how these can help us to better understand the complex interweaving of the actions of large numbers of people, and of planned and unplanned processes.

THE NATURE OF GAME MODELS

Game models are put forward by Elias to explore the question:

> How exactly does it come about that people, because of their interdependence and the way their actions and experience inter-mesh, form a type of figuration, a kind of order which is relatively autonomous from the type of order encountered if, like biologists or psychologists, one investigates individual people either as represent-atives of their species or as isolated persons?   (Elias, 1970, p. 72)

Elias sees game models as a possible vehicle for understanding the way in which human aims and actions intertwine by temporarily isolating them in close focus. They are meant as simplified analogies to real social processes which enable social scientists to map the complex figurations they seek to study but also map the games people think they are playing. The models are of contests which (in the simpler forms at least) resemble real games like chess, bridge, football or tennis. They represent contests played out – more or less – according to rules (Elias, 1970, p. 73).

The game models are offered as simplified analogies of more complex social processes. The models help to bring out more graphically the processual character of relationships between interdependent people while they also focus attention, in particular, on changing balances of power, or power-ratios, as a central aspect of the web of human relations; in this context it should be borne in mind that games are contests and that all the game models are based on two or more people measuring their strength against each other. Power, concep-tualized not as a property which one person or group has and another person or group does not have, but as a structural characteristic of all human relationships, is central to Elias's approach. Within the context of understanding processes of managed social change, the game models are useful precisely because they demonstrate that the outcomes of the complex interweaving of the actions of different players in the game, even where these actions are more or less consciously directed towards the attainment of certain goals, may include – in the case of complex games almost certainly will include – outcomes which no single player or group of players intended. Within the context of managing social change the 'game' is, of course, the game of implementing, or resisting the implementation of, a given policy strategy.

Elias's discussion of game models is prefaced by what he calls the primal contest, which is a far cry from a game in that it represents a real and deadly contest between two groups. Briefly he describes two tribes, both hunters and gatherers, who draw on the same land for food. Food is scarce and becoming scarcer as drought and other natural forces take their toll. The tribespeople do not understand why food continues to become scarcer. Conflict breaks out, one tribe raids the other and kills a number of its members and this tribe then retaliates. Elias argues this 'enduring antagonism' reveals itself as a form of functional interdependence because, as rivals for shrinking food resources, they are dependent on one another as in a game of chess (which was originally a war game). Each move of one group limits the possibilities of each move of the other group and vice-versa such that:

> The internal arrangements in each group are determined to a greater or lesser extent by what each group thinks the other might do next. Fierce antagonists, in other words, perform a function for each other, because the interdependence of human beings due to their hostility is no less a functional relationship than due to their position as friends, allies and specialists bonded to each other through the division of labour. (Elias, 1970, p. 77)

Elias's most simple game model involves just two people, one of whom is a much stronger player than the other. The stronger player can, to a very considerable degree, constrain the actions and limit the options of the weaker player to make certain moves, whereas the weaker player is much less able to constrain the actions of the stronger player. However, the weaker player does have some degree of control over the stronger for, in planning his or her own moves the stronger player has at least to take the weaker player's moves into account. In other words, in any game the participants always have, though in considerably varying degrees, some control over each other. Where the differential between the players' strengths in the game (that is the balance of power or their power-ratio) is very great, the stronger player has not only a higher degree of control over his or her opponent but also a higher degree of control over the game as such. The stronger player is thus able significantly to control the course of the game, not only by winning, but also by determining the manner of the victory and perhaps the length of time taken. In a very simple game of this kind, we are able to understand the course of the game largely in terms of the goals and plans of the stronger player.

However, let us now consider a two-person game in which the two players are of roughly equal ability (that is of roughly equal power). As the differential between the strength of the players decreases, so the ability of the stronger player to force the weaker player to make certain moves diminishes, as does the stronger player's ability to determine the course of the game. Correspondingly, the weaker player's control over the stronger player increases but, as the power balance between the two players becomes less unequal, so the course of the game increasingly passes beyond the control of either. As Elias put it:

> Both players will have correspondingly less chance to control the changing figuration of the game; and the less dependent will be the changing figuration of the game on the aims and plans for the course of the game which each player has formed by himself. The stronger, conversely, becomes the dependence of each of the two players' overall plans and of each of their moves on the changing figuration of the game – on the game process. The more the game comes to resemble a social process, the less it comes to resemble the implementation of an individual plan. In other words, to the extent that the inequality in the strengths of the two players diminishes, there will result from the interweaving of moves of two individual people a game process *which neither of them has planned.*
>
> (Elias, 1978, p. 82. Italics in original)

Elias considers a variety of game models from, in increasing order of complexity, multi-person games at one level (for example in which one player may be playing simultaneously against several other players, or in which two sides each containing several players compete against each other) through to multi-person, multi-level games. In this latter group of game models, the number of players increases and the structure of the game becomes increasingly complex. In particular, in multi-level games not all the players play directly with each other and moves may be made by specialized functionaries such as leaders, delegates, representatives, committees and governments, on an upper tier. In addition, while each side continues to struggle against the opposition, there may be more than two sides – indeed there may be many sides – involved in these games. Part of the increased complexity of the game relates to the fact that there are now several different balances of power which have to be taken into account: among the top-tier players; between the top and lower-tier players; and among lower-tier players. The balance of power between the upper-tier and lower-tier players may be relatively unequal, in which case there is a relatively oligarchic game structure, or it may be relatively equal, in which case the game is relatively democratic. It is these more complex game models which are most useful for shedding light on complex processes in modern societies, such as the processes involved in, for example, planning and managing processes of social change.

It is important to note that as the number of players and the complexity of the game increase, and as the power differentials between the players diminish, so the course of the game becomes increasingly unpredictable and increasingly beyond the ability of any single individual or group of players to control. It was noted earlier that in the case of a simple two-person game played between players of very unequal ability, the course of the game can be explained largely in terms of the plans and goals of the stronger player. However, as the number of interdependent players grows, it also becomes clear how little the game can be controlled and guided from any single player's or group's position; indeed the opposite is the case, for it becomes clear how much the course of the game – which is actually the product of the interweaving moves of a large number of players – increasingly constrains the moves of every single player. The development and direction of the game become more and more opaque to the individual player and, within this context, it becomes increasingly difficult for any player or group of players to put together an accurate mental picture of the course of the game as a whole. However strong the individual may be, he or she will become less and less able to control the moves of other players and the course of the game and, from the point of view of the individual player, an intertwining network of more and more players functions increasingly as though it had a life of its own. In summary, the game models, and in particular the more complex models:

indicate the conditions under which players may slowly begin to encounter a problem: that a game process, which comes about entirely as a result of the interweaving of the individual moves of many players, takes a course *which none of the individual players has planned, determined or anticipated.*   (Elias, 1978, p. 95)

A possible danger of using game models is that it would be easy to assume that rules are essential and it is the rules that pattern social life. If this assumption were made, then the game models would be open to the criticisms made of Parsons' consensual model of didactic interaction (Parsons, 1951); for example, the failure to deal with power and conflict and the fact that people do not enter social inter-action untouched by upbringing and previous social relationships. Elias's point is that there are always rules, however not all the players understand them in the same way. The empirical challenge is to understand the players' view of the rules and the areas of ambiguity. The primal contest demonstrates that it is not possible to explain the actions, plans and aims of groups if they are conceptualized as the freely chosen decisions, plans and aims of each group considered on its own, independently of the other group. It is only by considering the constraints the groups exert upon each other by reason of their inter-dependence, 'their bilateral function for each other as enemies', that an adequate explanation can be put forward.

THE UTILITY OF GAME MODELS

It is helpful to apply some of the insights offered by game models to the discussion of the formation and reorganization of the NHS in England and Wales contained in Chapter 2. To recap briefly, the organization of the NHS has moved from a situation where health services were delivered largely by the hospital-based medical profes-sion, as well as the mêlée of community and preventative care services, in a context of what were generally considered to be relatively ad-equate finances, to a situation where medicine's capacity to cure and prevent illness has improved such that the costs of providing health care has soared and, at the same time, the dominance of acute health services has become less and less appropriate for the population's changing health needs.

By the 1970s, government increasingly saw its task as seeking ways to curb the increasing costs of health care. The course of action open to government was by no means clear, partly because of lack of information about the effectiveness of various interventions and partly because of the numbers of interdependent groups involved in health care, most of whom had, and continue to have, differing views about the appropriateness and effectiveness of treatments, how health services ought to be delivered and who represented varying interest groups with a diversity of agendas and differing powers to influence health policy. (The strength of the medical profession *vis-à-vis* other occupational groups and indeed the profession's power to avoid accountability to the State has been well documented elsewhere (Jamous and Peloille, 1970; Johnson, 1972; Jewson, 1974; Larson, 1977; Waddington, 1984; Larkin, 1988).) For all of these reasons, governments have found it increasingly difficult to gain an accurate picture of how to improve the delivery of health care in order to ensure that it meets the often-stated, if unclear, criteria – effective, efficient and economical.

The overall figuration in the early 1970s is akin to what Elias calls the simplified increasingly democratic type. Groups and individuals in the NHS got on with administering health services in accordance with the demands of those who were the main spenders of the resources – doctors. A diverse range of groups also sought to improve their position in terms of status, pay and/or security. What occupational groups and the government seemed most unhappy about was that the medical profession had moved so far apart from other groups and was able to dictate how health care was delivered and was playing a game quite independently of every other group and according to different rules.

In an attempt to control the game, government adopted managerialism as a means of speech and thought to get some control over health services. However, the nature of managerialism has changed over time. As discussed in Chapter 2, bureaucracy was the dominant strategy devised to deal with the evolving pressures on the NHS in the 1970s, along with certain other themes; for example, devolution downwards, accountability upwards. Empirical studies of local health care management at this time demonstrate the ability of local health services to ignore the policies and priorities of the Centre, primarily because of the power of doctors to resist attempts to manage their activity and because of uncertainty as to how to change health services so that they met accepted priorities for health care.

These studies also highlight the relative strengths of different players. For example, we are told that the most influential actors after doctors are administrators, with the health authority and community groups lagging a good way behind. In these studies the Centre or region are depicted as players who have little influence on the periphery and are largely ignored as players. General management could be seen as another brand of managerialism adopted by the government to deal with the evolving pressures on the NHS and to try to gain control of a complex game.

To what extent can Elias's game models help explain the descriptive data presented in this chapter? In this respect it is helpful to begin to map out the figuration of which DGMs were a part. Crudely, such a map would be as shown in Figure 5.2. Figure 5.2 oversimplifies the complexity of the network in at least three ways. Firstly, it is a snapshot of a complex moving situation. Secondly, it focuses on the immediate chains of interdependence and there are no doubt other relationships which impact on the social context in which DGMs are a part. Finally, it takes no account of conditions specific to individual districts. An obvious point to make is that individual DGMs are situated in different figurations, where some actors are more powerful in some districts than others. It follows therefore, that DGMs' priorities and actions will be different, depending on the figuration of which they are a part. For example, a powerful chair meant that one DGM, a former industrialist, spent significantly less time on health authority business and district management than others in the sample because his main task was trying to find out what the chair was doing (the chair spent five days a week in the district) and fighting to establish his own authority within the district. Furthermore, the ability of a DGM to take a detour *via* detachment with respect to doctors seems to improve the influence they had with the profession and the activity of doctors.

This map of a figuration adds weight to a central point made during the review of the existing empirical studies of local management of health services, namely that it is not possible to explain the actions, plans and aims of people if they are conceptualized as the freely-chosen decisions, plans and aims of each person or group considered on their own, independently of other people. An adequate explanation requires, at a minimum, that investigators consider the constraints each group exerts upon others by reason of their interdependence.

The figuration of interdependent players is the framework for the game. Quite simply, it is the existence of other players which serves to muddy the rules of the game for the general manager. Particularly powerful in this respect are the government, medical profession and its

115

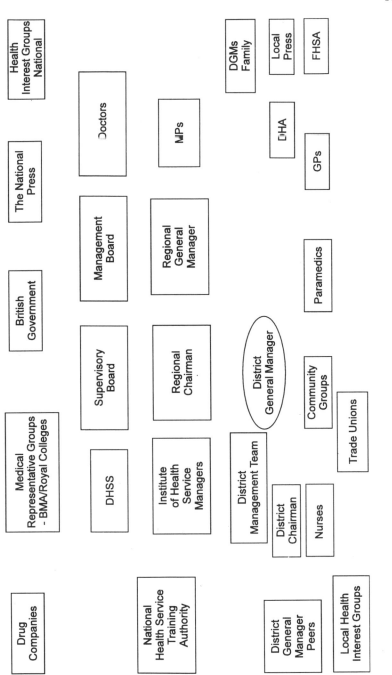

Figure 5.2 A typical figuration for a District General Manager

representative groups, the press (national and local) and MPs. Figure 5.3 attempts to consider the power balances of key players within the figuration, though, again, it should be noted that this is an over-simplification. For example, there will also be relationships between trade unions and paramedics, between MPs and the local press and so on, though it would be impossible to represent all possible relation-ships diagrammatically.

Doctors and their professional bodies have a wide array of powerful arguments that can be marshalled to counter health policy and prior-ities for health services; for example, those concerned with increasing community care and preventive health services, and reducing acute services. Doctors may cite individual cases where a patient has not been able to have access to expensive treatment because of inadequate health care budgets, or they may publicize the existence of advanced medical technology that could have prolonged a patient's life if only the funds had been made available. Such arguments have a significant emotional impact and are beloved of the press who, in narrating such cases, may stir up local communities and MPs to bring individual cases to the attention of Parliament and, in so doing, may scupper a district's spending plans geared towards meeting the evolving health needs of the district population.

Health interest groups also lobby government and use the press to influence policy. This dynamic at the higher-tier has profound effects on district management and on the web of social relationships within the districts. It means that planning and issues of strategy are open to compromise at any time. Furthermore, managing change is vastly more difficult. Another profound higher-tier influence on district management is the time-honoured tradition of changing either fund-ing projections for health care or some aspect of health policy in order to win support of voters as a general election looms large, and again the press – a game player almost wholly beyond the control of local health service managers – is centrally involved.

The findings about district general management as reported in this chapter suggest that dealing with this higher-tier dynamic takes a great deal of the DGMs' time, and one consequence of this is that very little time and effort is spent with what Elias would term lower-tier players such as nurses, community groups, GPs, trades unions, local authorities and paramedics. Even though these groups may be valued by individual DGMs, they are not powerful enough to influ-ence the DGMs' agenda and hence remain largely ignored. Further-more, dealing with the higher-tier dynamic means that variable time is

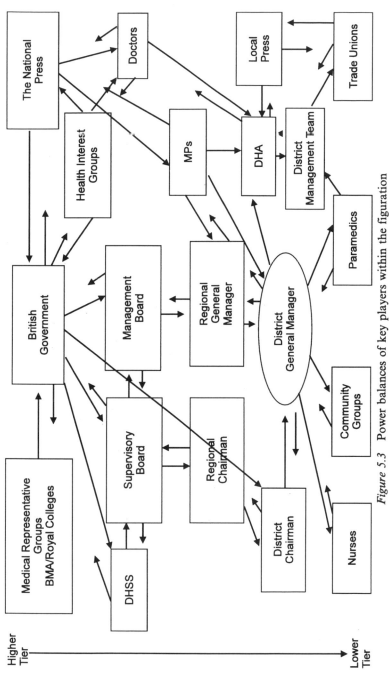

Figure 5.3 Power balances of key players within the figuration

Note: Length of arrow signifies the power of people/groups in this figuration.

spent on the DHA, often depending on either its composition (for example in one district a prospective MP as a member of the DHA meant general management had to spend a great deal of time on this relationship, while in another district a predominantly Labour health authority used DHA meetings to voice their dislike of Tory policies) or competence or the power of the chair over the membership or the DGM.

However, it is important to recognize that despite the relative powerlessness of lower-tier players to impact on the DGMs' agenda, they do have some power. For example, it was noted earlier in this chapter that although the DHA was in the main perceived by DGMs in this sample to be a cumbersome, largely ineffective body, the existence of the DHA did influence the way in which DGMs worked and was a factor in their decisions as to what type of work to concentrate on.

The point of game models is not just that they facilitate a relatively detached description of the situation as seen by social scientists, but they also enable one to explore the games players think they are playing, or try to persuade other people to play. Drawing on the fieldwork data presented here, it is possible, albeit crudely, to tease out players' appreciation of the complexity of the social relationships of which they are a part, and to examine their own views of the game.

The formally-stated object of the game – which in this case is a policy process game – is that players should engage in forms of action that substantially improve the health of the population of the UK and the quality of health care delivery, whilst ensuring that public funds are used so that value for money is delivered. However, players may have different and varied opinions as to how these laudable objectives are to be achieved. Moreover, they may not see these issues as the most important and they may also define terms such as 'efficiency' and 'effectiveness' very differently. In this case, although all players are nominally playing the same game, there may be 'games within games' with different groups having different agendas, each seeking to impose their agenda on others. The 'games within the game' of the key NHS players are discussed below, albeit in a simplified fashion. It should be noted that some players play games independently of others.

The game for the Centre (government, management board, supervisory board) is affected by a desire to keep clear of the press, deal with a myriad of powerful interest groups who lobby the Centre at every opportunity, and make sure the pot of public money is not swallowed up by health care. Recognizing the public's affection for the NHS, those at the Centre also clearly wish to avoid any criticism of their handling of health policy or of the management of health services. Those at the Centre need, therefore, to ensure that health services are delivered in accordance with these points and have tried with every NHS reorganization to gain a level of control over this process.

Those people working at the region, and the RGM in particular, were involved in a difficult balancing act – that is, balancing what is expected of them as agents of the Centre with their accountability to a large population represented by a regional chair and RHA who are, in the main, political appointments.

DHA members often saw general management as increasing the power of the district chair at their expense. Furthermore, the majority of members saw their districts as being squeezed financially by the region and the Centre. The game for them, therefore, involves trying to preserve their powers in the policy-making process.

Doctors, on the whole, rejected the objectives of the game, and sought to continue to play an historically much older game in which the dominance of the doctors was a central aspect. They preferred to deal with the district chair rather than the DGM if concerned with a managerial issue, indicating their views of where the power to change lies. Managers varied in the extent to which they tried to engage doctors in management's game.

CHCs saw the game, following the introduction of general management, as being one designed to reduce community involvement in the planning and delivery of health services. People working for the CHC fought against a centrally driven health service which they believed was unlikely to be responsive to local needs.

Nurses saw the game as being characterized by 'unfair' rules which placed them at a disadvantage. They resented the threat general management constituted to their hard-won professional status and they also resented being managed by non-nurses.

These summaries of some views of the game are generalizations and are data to be explained. In order to understand the game, it is important not to see the Griffiths reorganization as simply an implementation of a plan, as a wholly rational process. Rather the game is a complex social process involving both cognitively-based and emotional resistances to change and an interweaving of the actions of many different groups in such a way that the outcome will almost certainly not be one which was intended by any one group. This may be seen even in the simplest game-models, for example the outcome of two chess players striving to defeat each other may actually be a stalemate. If this can happen even in very simple two-person games, then it is even more likely – indeed almost inevitable – that in complex games such as that involved in reorganizing a huge and complex organization like the NHS there were outcomes which no-one intended.

The next chapter attempts to take the arguments developed so far in the book and apply them to a more specific example of one DGM's attempt to manage change in his district.

6 Case Study: The Development of a Mental Health Policy

INTRODUCTION

This chapter documents how a District General Manager (DGM) sought to improve mental health services in his district and the problems he encountered. The analysis counterposes the DGM's relatively involved perception of these problems with an understanding of these problems as revealed by a relatively detached, sociological analysis. The case study is intended to illuminate the process-sociological approach which, it has been argued, is helpful in understanding a common aspect of managed change, namely unplanned outcomes.[1]

THE DISTRICT

The mental health services provided by the DHA are centred on three large sites and three smaller sites. Part of the strategic plan for the district was to reduce services to two main sites. There are no long-stay mental illness or mental handicap hospitals in the district, psychiatric services being provided within two medium-sized hospitals, one at each end of the district. However, the district has to plan for the development of community services to receive 'clients' from neighbouring districts. The resident population is 308 000 and there are five consultant psychiatrists in post.

THE DGM

The DGM was in his early 40s. Following a natural science first degree and a doctorate in metallurgy, he held a variety of general management posts in manufacturing industries. Richard (a pseudonym), described himself as 'a high energy person who likes causing people to work' and whose 'natural penchant is to think long-term and get the broad things going'. He sees his particular skills lying in the selection of key items for change – 'exploiting pockets of opportunity and testing out possibilities' – as well as listening to the views of others.

BACKGROUND TO THE DEVELOPMENT OF THE STRATEGY

The DHA was obliged to resettle up to 70 residents of a long-stay psychiatric hospital. The district had no psychiatric hospitals itself, and has in the past transferred those people in need of long-term care to hospitals outside the district. There were 121 acute beds, 134 elderly beds, 45 rehabilitation beds (300 in total), and 244 day-hospital places for adults and for the elderly in psychiatry.

In the district under examination, the development of a comprehensive mental health strategy became a priority partly as a consequence of actions by key players outside of the district, for the mental health services in the district had recently been severely criticized in a report from the Health Advisory Service (HAS), while the Royal College of Psychiatrists had also expressed concern about the quality of training available within the district. The DGM saw the development of a mental health strategy as a means not only of improving the embarrassingly poor mental health services in the district, but also as a means of demonstrating the effectiveness of the new management structure. Together with a core group of his senior managers, the DGM developed a strategy which centred on five services/client groups: acute psychiatric services, rehabilitation, services for the elderly mentally ill, child and adolescent psychiatry, and drug and alcohol abuse. The strategy as a whole involved a shift away from hospital-based towards community-based care, and a central aspect of the strategy involved the resettlement in the community of some 70 residents of a long-stay psychiatric hospital. This resettlement programme was central to the plan to re-shape the service, not least because it was to provide the additional resources needed to build up the community-based services.

Throughout the process of developing and implementing the mental health strategy, the complex discussions and negotiations in which the DGM and his core management team were involved with groups both inside and outside the district were monitored. Following the implementation of the strategy, and at my request, the DGM wrote a brief evaluation of the implementation of the mental health strategy. He acknowledged that the strategy had had very limited success in effecting a shift away from hospital-based and towards community-based services, largely because the plan to resettle some 70 residents of a long-stay psychiatric hospital – which was, as we have noted, central to the success of the wider strategy – had been vigorously opposed, in particular, by psychiatric consultants and by some groups within the local community. As a consequence, only 14 patients were resettled in a local hostel and a further seven in a terraced house in the district. Of equal sociological interest, however, is the fact that it is possible to identify a number of unintended consequences – of which more will be said shortly – none of which was mentioned by the DGM in his own evaluation of the strategy and of which he seemed to be either unaware or, at best, only partially aware.

THE PRODUCTION OF THE STRATEGY

There was general dissatisfaction with the psychiatric services prior to the development of the strategy. The psychiatrists were by no means satisfied with the service they provided, complaining of 'a lack of resources', a comment echoed by other professional staff. The psychiatrists, in particular, wanted a 'better library' and most vociferously campaigned for 'more wards and beds'. They were anxious to ensure that sites where services were provided were of equal status with respect to beds, and were particularly unhappy with the local authority's provision of Part 3 accommodation. However, in the DGMs view, this accommodation was essential for a balanced mental health service. It comprises part-supervised community-based homes for those who cannot manage on their own and yet whose condition does not warrant longer care in a hospital setting. Richard believed that part of the reason for the consultant psychiatrists' dissatisfaction with the Part 3 accommodation was that the patients would not be effectively under their control, as they would be in hospital.

The nursing profession were also unhappy with the service as it then existed, complaining that they were denied a 'proper voice' in the provision of the service. The paramedic professions also believed their opinions to be 'devalued, particularly by the doctors' and were particularly frustrated because they were unable to provide the service where their skills could be utilized. The local authority were also dissatisfied with the relationship with the health authority which, in their view, hindered service provision. The local authority believed the DHA to be 'too secretive', investing too little in mental health – both in beds and in community staff – and to be lacking in any sense of direction or drive for the mental health service.

Another group dissatisfied with the service as it was then organized was the DHA. The independent HAS report which had severely criticized the district had shocked the members of the health authority who had not appreciated the severity of the problem. The Royal College of Psychiatrists had also expressed their dissatisfaction with the status of training within the district and had threatened to take action unless a significant improvement occurred. Rather surprisingly, neither the CHC nor the National Association for Mental Health (MIND) were involved in seeking change.

Three months into his job, Richard took what he described as an 'intuitive decision to act'. He spoke of 'a need to do something', particularly to respond to the critical HAS report, and of 'wanting to perform in the light of the regional requirements for resettlement'. He did not seek advice at this point because 'I knew if I did, nothing would have happened'. Richard wanted to establish himself as 'the general manager and as someone who could bring about change'. He saw the reform and improvement of the mental health services as 'an opportunity for a big bang approach' which would fulfil several of his objectives:

- to enhance his credibility as a manager in the eyes of region and the DHA;
- to show the district the potential of general management to achieve change;
- to show that general management constituted a significant improvement on the old system of consensus management;
- to improve the embarrassingly poor mental health services; and
- to give a sense of direction to the consultant psychiatrists and 'win over consultant opinion'.

His desire for change coincided with the appointment of a new male Director of Nursing Service (DNS), described by Richard as 'bright and innovative' and 'fired with enthusiasm' for a particular approach to community care which he had helped introduce in his last job. He canvassed the DGM to adopt this approach in the district and used his recent experience to argue that the district services could be run in a 'different and more effective way'. Richard was struck by the DNSs passion and enthusiasm for the project and said: 'I saw the DNS as the instrument to implement, review and change the mental health services'.

He decided to make the DNS project manager for the mental health strategy. Project management was an approach Richard had been particularly keen to introduce into his district on his arrival as it had been a management tool he had successfully used in his previous job in the private sector. The DNS was charged with the task of managing the project. At the time Richard claimed, 'Griffiths didn't really enter my mind, I was driven by my own approach to management'. Nevertheless it provided an essential backcloth for his actions and, whether he realized it or not, may have been associated with the hostility of the psychiatrists towards management. The strategy had also become Richard's 'vehicle to change the relationships with doctors'.

The need for improvement of the mental health services of the district, and for action, was conveyed to the psychiatric division during a routine meeting to discuss the HAS report. No real commitment to change was sought from the consultant psychiatrists at this stage as it was felt 'to be self-evident that something must be done'. The chair of the psychiatric division, a psychiatrist, was, Richard admitted, 'told rather than asked' to be involved in the planning and restructuring of mental health services. He went on to say: 'there was never a sense of going to the psychiatrist with the HAS report and saying "what will we do about it?". I took command of the situation and said "something must be done" '. Richard later suggested that this was possibly the start of the rift with the chair of the psychiatric division. Richard assumed him to be enthusiastic about a change in the direction of the service following his display of interest at a 'change planning conference' held in the September following Richard's appointment at which he outlined some of the changes he hoped to bring to the district – his 'vision of the future'.

With the approval and support of his top management team, Richard formed a core group which was charged with the task of formulating a draft strategy for a district comprehensive mental health service covering the range of mental health problems. The core group was kept deliberately small because Richard wanted to avoid what he saw as the problems of the old NHS where, because everyone was represented on the management team, nothing got done. As he said: 'I went for a small core team to get a positive course of action which would then be "sold" to the rest of the organization'. It consisted of a specialist in community medicine, the health authority chair, a consultant psychiatrist, the then district administrator, the assistant director of social services, and the DNS-psychiatry, who was the project manager. A GP representative for the core group was invited but no name was put forward.

The planned strategy was divided into five services/client groups:

1. *Acute*, meeting the needs of people who require crisis intervention, assessment, acute psychiatric illness, mental health education and prevention.
2. *Rehabilitation* for people with demonstrable psychiatric illness which is likely to cause them difficulties in living independently in the community. Skilled care and specialized services needed to be developed to meet these needs.
3. *Elderly mentally ill*, in particular people who have psychiatric problems associated with ageing. The service here was to focus on community support, early recognition of psychiatric problems and inadequate accommodation in the community, backed up by assessment facilities and some long-stay care in in-patient units.
4. *Child and adolescent psychiatry*, a specialist service for people under the age of 18.
5. *Drug and alcohol abuse*, a specialised community-based service for people with problems related to alcohol and drug abuse.

This was the first time in the district's history that the district mental health services had been considered as a whole, and it was the first time that such an approach had been undertaken in the region concerned, by a 'receiving' district. Richard argued that this was a reflection of the weakness of the previous psychiatric unit management group (consisting of a unit administrator, a consultant and a nurse), formed following the 1982 reorganization, and poor regional management. In addition to these changes, the strategy sought to address the resettlement of the long-stay patients, and create a balanced, comprehensive service involving both District General Hospital (DGH)-based facilities and community-based facilities.

Richard hoped that the strategy would be available six months later for consideration by the DHA and the local authority. To assist in this planning of a major programme of change, the services of a change-management consultant from the NHS Training Authority (NHSTA) were purchased. Richard asked the core group to establish, in a two-day workshop, the base 'philosophy' for the strategy which outlined the requirements for a comprehensive mental health service and was kept informed primarily by the DNS-psychiatry as project manager.

The strategy formation team felt that in order to provide an effective mental health service, the service should be:

- *Local* The service was to be organized to serve natural population groups of about 40–60 000 people. This was to be achieved by dividing the coterminous boundaries of health and social services into six localities, which matched the existing internal localities of the local authority.
- *Accessible* The service was to be organized so that people in each locality would be aware of the service that was being provided. Whilst existing methods of access into the service were to be maintained, a variety of different ways of access were to be developed to meet the different needs of individual clients. The community mental health resource centre (a resource within the community that deals with referred mental health problems and coordinates the delivery of mental health services for the catchment area) was to act as the focus for their development and people could present 'from the street'. Resource centres were to be staffed by a team of people, including a social worker, community psychiatric nurses and a psychiatrist.
- *Comprehensive* The service was to be planned to meet the whole range of mental health problems.

The core group decided that the detailed strategy would need the involvement of others who were themselves involved in the delivery of mental health services. Five sub-groups of the core team were established to develop a strategy for each client group (adult, child and adolescent, rehabilitation, drug and alcohol abuse and the elderly).

Each of the consultant psychiatrists was invited by the chair of the division to lead one of the five sub-groups. (The consultant on the core team was excluded from this with his agreement.) A member of the core group was assigned to one of the five sub-groups to provide consistency of interpretation and views between the core group statement of principles and the sub-group consideration. As a result, around 100 people were involved in the formation of the strategy from a range of different disciplines and organizations, including consultant psychiatrists, social workers, community psychiatric nurses, hospital nurses, occupational therapists, hospital nurses, psychologists, GPs, paramedical professionals, CHC members and the voluntary sector. Three of the five consultants took up a responsibility to lead the sub-groups. Richard believed the failure of two consultants to assume leadership roles to be the result of 'the chair of the division's weakness in management terms and his failure to explain the importance of the involvement of the consultants in each group'. No attempt was made by management to make any further effort to involve the consultants in the sub-groups because Richard felt he could not 'command them to participate... so there was no point fighting a battle I was certain to lose'.

Each sub-group produced the recommendations for their service developments within the philosophy statement of the core group, but without any financial statement. The chair of the core group, the Senior Physician in Community Medicine (SCM) and the strategy implementation manager (the DNS), put together these ideas to form a compendium which was compatible with the original philosophy statement and met the deadline set by Richard. The DGM was pleased with the compendium, but as it was not yet a costed strategy it was said not to be suitable for formal external consultation. This was the 'official' reason. Unofficially, Richard was concerned about the quality and viability of the sub-group strategies. In practice many of the sub-groups met once, probably twice. The consultant psychiatrist who headed one of the sub-groups produced a document that was inappropriate because it was hospital-based only and was in fact rewritten by the DNS.

An internal period of consultation was undertaken using the compendium-of-ideas document. In parallel with this, a manpower and financial analysis was carried out. It was during this phase that Richard noted the first overt signs of a lack of commitment on the part of the psychiatrists. During the writing of the sub-strategies, the chair of the division withdrew from his involvement in the strategy without officially giving any notice. Richard and some of his colleagues attributed this response to peer-group pressures. The chair of the division's association with the core group led to accusations of betrayal from his colleagues. His colleagues saw the development of a community-based service to be a direct and very real threat to psychiatric beds. The chair of the division attacked the strategy in a letter, thus gaining favour with his psychiatric colleagues. In the letter (on behalf of his colleagues), he highlighted the essential elements of a 'successful strategy' which included compatibility with national trends, compatibility with the regional strategy ensuring a specialist orientation, appropriateness to local needs and acceptability to the profession.

This letter was received some 10 days after the closing date for internal consultation, a process which had yielded comments which were mainly favourable. The strategy, as a result of the points put forward in the letter, missed the target DHA meeting. This is in itself an interesting indicator of power. Subsequently, a seminar to present the strategy was arranged for members. The consultant psychiatrist (the original member of the core group but no longer chair of the division) spoke out vehemently against the strategy in his presentation, much to the surprise of the DHA and the DGM who assumed that the strategy was agreed. Richard argued at this point that his assumption as to the cooperative stance of the psychiatrists was based on the consultant's 'participation in the core group'. At the heart of the presentation of the consultant's objections was a complaint of lack of involvement. Other complaints included the inadequacy of the local authority provision, the inadequacies of the DGH-based facilities, and the claim that community psychiatry was an unproven method of service delivery. Underlying these objections was a concern about the building of a 'resource centre', one of six planned, which were seen as a threat to hospital-based provision.

At the time Richard felt the lead consultant psychiatrist had 'stabbed him in the back', because of his desire to rebuild his status with his colleagues. The only objection Richard considered to be valid was the inadequacy of the local authority provision. He planned to retrieve the commitment of the psychiatrists. He was under pressure to do so because of a high profile national conference and presentation of the strategy which had been planned for three months' time, backed by some regional funding. The conference day was retitled to accommodate the consultant's concern. It was no longer a launch of an agreed statement, but renamed 'Mental Health Services in Transition'.

Richard decided against any personal involvement in dealing with the psychiatrists' objections for fear of being accused of self-interest, and because of a genuine feeling of vulnerability in discussions of issues of clinical need. In order to keep the momentum of change going, he assigned to the SCM and the strategy implementation manager (the DNS) the task of talking to the psychiatrists individually, hoping that this would resolve their objections.

Meanwhile, plans for resettlement and rehabilitation of mental illness patients, in line with the regional strategy and separate from the district strategy, went ahead. To meet HAS criticisms of overcrowding on the hospital wards, a proposal was developed by the DNS to reduce the beds in one hospital and to compensate by using three nearby houses (owned by the DHA) to provide 11 places for people in the process of being rehabilitated. The local community complained strongly, public meetings were held, and the management were forced to reconsider the plan. The DHA had not been informed of the proposed use of the three houses, and when it hit the press the DGM was criticized and regretted his error. 'I didn't realise its potential in the public arena'. This incident led to claims that the mental health strategy was being implemented before it was agreed. In particular, the consultant psychiatrists argued the incident was a clear indication that the strategy was designed to take away some of the beds in their charge. Richard, however, saw the problem as a misunderstanding and a confusion between the existing regional strategy, which was to happen regardless of any initiative pursued independently by the district and the new mental health strategy.

The consultants' irate reaction was seen by Richard as an indication that his attempts to retrieve the commitment of the psychiatrists via the SCM and DNS had failed. He attributed this to the personalities involved. The SCM, he argued, 'lacked the assertiveness necessary to engage the consultants in a realistic dialogue', and the DNS failed to pick up any signs of dissention because of his 'unbridled enthusiasm'. Indeed, Richard admitted:

Looking back on it, I was not sensitive to this unbridled optimism in him. I wanted to hear that the problems had been overcome so I chose to let it remain in my subconscious.

The conference itself went well. Members, representatives from the region and the professions attending, seemed to respond favourably. The 'soft objective' for the conference, to improve the district's public image, was, according to the DGM, achieved. The refined consultation document, refined in the sense that it was now a costed strategy (in terms of finance and personnel), was put to the DHA and a formal consultation process began. In the middle of this process the DNS-psychiatry was headhunted for another job. Despite this loss, the DGM was confident things were 'going well' and remarked on the success of joint planning. The UGM of hospital X and the community unit, a former unit administrator from another district, was regarded by Richard and his chair as 'the natural successor' to oversee the implementation of the strategy because of his experience in working in the community sector.

At the end of the second consultation period, lasting some two months, the received responses were positive with the exception of those from the local medical committee (the GP body). This committee, chaired by the GP representative on the management group of the DHA, was largely apathetic. Richard described this GP as 'the only shop steward I have met in doctoring terms'. He had always opposed the strategy from an 'ideological' standpoint, was unwilling to join the core group and, medically, saw it as a threat to the independence of GPs. Richard believed the GP falsely perceived that this was a 'management written strategy'.

A week after the closing date, a letter from the psychiatrists arrived, reiterating their previous objections, the main one again being loss of beds. The strategy missed the DHA meeting, instead responses were presented at the DHA meeting. At this juncture the DGM saw the DHA as 'having to make a decision whether to back the medical view or that of general management, supported by representatives of consumer groups and other professions who had made favourable responses to the consultation document'.

The UGM community and the DGM met with the consultants to try to sort out the issue of bed levels. The SCM was consulted on this issue, although not present in the discussions with the psychiatrists because of her perceived ineffectiveness by the DGM in the previous round of discussions. The DGM and UGM felt that they had gone as far as they could to 'explain the strategy to consultants', 'to obtain their understanding that the strategy was in the best interest of the service' and 'that it was in their interest to support it'. The matter, they argued, had to be put to the DHA without the support of the consultants. Richard tried to 'rebuild bridges' with the consultants by negotiating with the region's treasurer that £35 000 be channelled into the district's psychiatric services from the region, an amount put by to fund a vacant sixth consultant psychiatrist post.

On the day of the special health authority meeting to discuss the strategy, the consultants asked to see the chair of the DHA. The chair gave total support to the DGM in his objectives for mental health services in the district, but according to Richard, 'found a means of allowing the strategy to proceed with the psychiatrists' qualified support'. In particular, he offered to look at the hospital bed requirements again and to monitor the community resource centre during its first year of operation. To consolidate the 'good will' the chair and the DGM invited the new chair of the psychiatric division to sit on the appointments panel for the new DNS-psychiatry. This agreement was written down and read out at the beginning of a special DHA meeting. The strategy was then supported by the DHA, formally approved at the next meeting, and implementation proceeded.

WHY PROBLEMS?

In seeking to understand the way in which the mental health strategy was developed and implemented, it is useful to draw upon Elias's game models. In particular, the model of a complex game involving many players (or groups of players) on several levels helps to highlight two centrally important points which it is helpful to bear in mind when studying the policy process. The first of these is that in complex games there are likely to be not merely two sides, but several sides, and – except in very rare situations where some players are able to stand back and take a relatively detached view of the game – players will normally find it difficult to understand the course of the game as a whole, but will have a more limited understanding of the game from their own perspective. As noted earlier, it is important to emphasize that games are contests and that the game models are trials of strength, and in this respect the game models help to steer us away from consensualist models of management, and to emphasize the fact that, particularly within complex organizations, different groups are likely to pursue what they perceive as their own interests, and that these may or may not coincide, or may coincide only very partially, with the perceived self-interests of other groups.

This point may be illustrated by reference to the case study. On a simple level, one might say that the objective of the mental health strategy was to develop a better mental health service. However, such a statement is underpinned by consensualist assumptions, and if we begin to ask what this meant to the many groups involved then we begin to understand the complexity of the situation and some of the tensions and conflicts which were involved. As noted, the proposed move towards a more community-based service was resisted by the psychiatrists, who saw it as a very direct and real threat to the continued provision of psychiatric beds. For them, a 'better' mental health service was one which maintained and expanded their already powerful position as the dominant group within this health care area;

a 'better' service, in their view, would involve not the loss of hospital beds, but the provision of more facilities to improve the quality of care in hospitals which were, of course, a major power base for the psychiatrists.

On the other hand, a 'better' service for the paramedical (for example community nursing) and social services professions was one which would allow them to play a fuller part in the treatment process which had traditionally been jealously guarded by the psychiatrists; hence there was a general welcome by the former for community-based care. For many members of the local community, who perceived the plan to relocate long-term patients in the community as a potential threat to the peace and security of local people, a 'better' mental health service was one which kept mental patients in secure accommodation away from the community. And for the DGM and his management team, a 'better' service was one which offered what they considered to be 'good value for money', which was in line with the policy of the government and the Regional Health Authority to develop community care and which would, in addition, demonstrate their own effectiveness and that of the new management structure.

The second point to which a complex game model draws attention is that the game is played by players on several different levels, or tiers, and that while all players are interdependent and therefore constrain each others' actions, higher-tier players have more power over lower-tier players than vice versa. In addition, it is important to note that upper-tier players do not necessarily play directly with lower-tier players. Thus, for example, in this case study upper-tier players outside the district, such as members of the Health Advisory Service or members of the Royal College of Psychiatrists, did not play directly with lower-tier players such as community nurses or members of the local community, though the actions of the latter were nevertheless significantly constrained by those of the former.

Players on the top tier were all located outside of the district level and included, in addition to members of the Health Advisory Service and the Royal College of Psychiatrists, those involved in the formulation of health care policy at the national government and Regional Health Authority levels. As already noted, a major constraint on the newly appointed DGM to develop a mental health care strategy came from the adverse report from the Health Advisory Service, coupled with pressure from the Royal College of Psychiatrists. Within the district, the DGM and his senior managers were top-tier players, along with the chair and other members of the District Health

Authority and, of central importance, the psychiatrists. Lower-tier players included members of the paramedical professions, local authority social workers, the Community Health Council, voluntary sector organizations, including the National Association for Mental Health (MIND) and, of course, lay members of the local community. Figure 6.1 is a diagramatic representation of the 'game' during the development of the mental health strategy. The figuration of inter-dependent players and of the game which they play together, is the framework for each individual move. Again, the diagram necessarily oversimplifies a very complex and dynamic process.

The complexity of the NHS, in terms of the number of groups involved and in terms of the shifting balances of power between those groups, means that any process of change is likely to involve a challenge to the self-perceived interests of one group or another. It is also important to emphasize that the capacity of some groups to shape or to resist change is greater than that of others. In the case study it was the psychiatrists who were at the district level the most powerful group and, insofar as any group emerged as 'winners', it is probably fair to say that it was they who, by virtue of their more or less successful resistance to the resettlement strategy, did so.

It is worth saying a little more about the involvement of the psy-chiatrists in the policy process. As described, during the early period of the formation of the policy – and despite the efforts of the DGM to involve them in this process – the psychiatrists played only a limited role. For the most part they chose not to become involved in what they saw as a relatively low status and largely administrative activity, and preferred to concentrate on what, in their view, they were trained to do, what they enjoyed doing and what they were paid to do: doctoring. However, as they began to perceive the emerging policy as a threat to their interests they became increasingly involved in the policy process, and though psychiatrists are perhaps one of the less powerful groups within the medical profession they were, within this figuration, still relatively powerful. On several occasions their refusal to cooperate delayed approval of the emerging strategy, and they also frequently by-passed the DGM and made their objections to the strategy known directly to the chair of the District Health Authority.

In making these objections they were able to draw upon well-rehearsed arguments involving an emphasis on clinical autonomy, the importance of trained medical opinion and the erosion of beds. Their intervention in this policy process came, as noted, relatively late, signifying their general lack of interest in management issues. How-

135

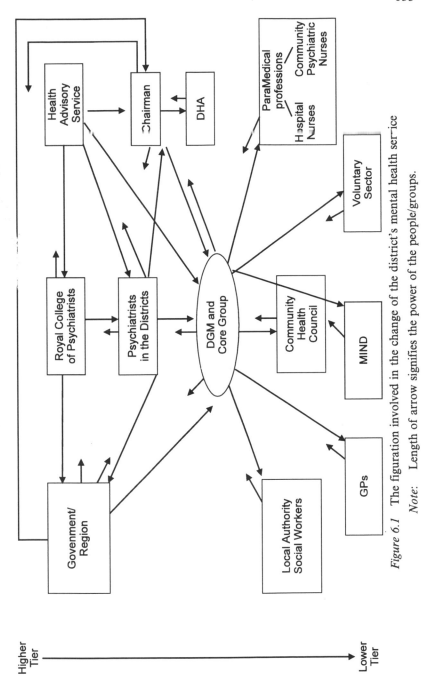

Higher
Tier

Lower
Tier

Figure 6.1 The figuration involved in the change of the district's mental health service

Note: Length of arrow signifies the power of the people/groups.

ever, the consequences of their intervention, when it came, were an index of their power in this figuration. It is significant that several groups of lower-tier players played a significant role in the early stages of the consultation process and were key players until the psychiatrists' concerns came to the fore, at which point the lower-tier status of the other players became very clear, and their ability to influence the policy process became much reduced.

It is also important to bear in mind that balances of power are not fixed and unchanging but that, on the contrary, they are continually in flux. This means that it should not be assumed that lower-tier players are always more or less passive spectators of a game which is played out, as it were, above their heads; for all players have some power, and lower-tier players may under certain circumstances – for example, insofar as scattered and relatively disorganized lower-tier players become increasingly united and better organized – significantly increase their power chances *vis-à-vis* some upper-tier players. A case in point was provided in the case study by those sections of the local community who, not without success, opposed the resettlement of psychiatric patients in the community.

Within the NHS, local communities are represented, in a formal sense, by CHCs. In this case the local community, through the CHC, was consulted about the mental health stategy in the time-honoured tradition of the NHS, namely through the receipt of a weighty strategy document. However, the DGM did not receive *via* the CHC any indication of the widespread anger within the community about the proposal to use three local houses to rehouse the psychiatric patients. This suggests not only that the CHC did not represent the local community very effectively but also that, at least in the early stages of the policy process, local community groups, as lower-tier players, were largely ignored by the district management team.

However, local residents developed their own *ad hoc* organization to campaign against the resettlement proposal. Public meetings were organized, the local press became involved and the DGM, who admitted that he was taken by surprise by the strength of the community's opposition, was forced to reconsider – and eventually substantially to amend – the strategy. It should of course be remembered that members of the local community were not alone in campaigning against the resettlement programme for, as we have noted, this programme was also opposed, for rather different reasons, by the psychiatrists. However, the fact that the local community played an important part in undermining the resettlement strategy serves as an important reminder that even lower-tier players are not wholly powerless.

The case study serves to illustrate a number of points relevant to the thrust of this book. The first of these is that the policy process rarely follows the neat, rational models of change set out in some of the management literature (for a review of the theoretical approaches to managing change, see Legge, 1984, and Spurgeon, 1991). Attempts to change policy are considerably more complex and messy than this literature suggests and are almost always characterized by unintended outcomes. In the case of the mental health strategy it should be noted that the strategy had been developed by the DGM and his team with a view to achieving a number of objectives, including the following:

- shifting the balance of care away from a hospital-based service;
- developing the local community as a resource in the provision of psychiatric care;
- reducing the centrality of psychiatrists and increasing the involvement of the para- and social work professions in the provision of care; and
- helping to establish the DGM's authority in his new role by demonstrating the effectiveness of the new management structure in bringing about significant improvements in care – by no means an unimportant consideration.

However, the development and implementation of the strategy resulted in a number of outcomes some of which were more or less the opposite of those which had originally been intended. These unintended outcomes included the following:

- the power of doctors to influence the outcome of change was emphasized;
- the continued importance of the 'hospital approach' to mental health services was emphasized;
- many members of the local community became more antagonistic towards plans for care in the community;
- members of the para-professions and social services were marginalized and disaffected;
- the power of the chair of the DHA was emphasized at the expense of both the DGM and ordinary members of the DHA; and
- the authority of the DGM and the value of the new management structure were called into question, not just by those who were

disappointed at the outcome and who felt that the consultation process had been a sham, but also by those – notably the psychiatrists and the local community – who had a greater influence on the outcome but between whom, and with the DGM, relationships also became very strained.

The case study also illustrates several points which were made earlier. Unanticipated outcomes of the kind outlined above are a consequence of the complex interweaving of the actions of large numbers of people pursuing their own goals, but – as is almost always the situation in complex games involving large numbers of players – with no single group being sufficiently powerful to control the course of the game. Closely associated with the inability of any single group to control the game is the fact that, as the game becomes increasingly complex, it also becomes increasingly difficult for any single player or group of players to develop an accurate picture of the game as a whole, and each player is likely to have only a very partial understanding of the game from his or her own perspective.

This leads on to a further important implication of the case study, which is that people who are involved in developing and implementing policies rarely understand fully the constraints within which either they or other key players work; as a consequence they frequently misunderstand, or at best only very partially understand, the actions and intentions of other players. For example, part of the case study research involved asking some of the key players, including the DGM, other senior managers and the consultant psychiatrists, for their views on why the development of the new policy had encountered so many difficulties. These views are documented below.

Why Change was Difficult – The DGM's View

Richard saw the main problems in individualistic terms, centring on the difficult personalities of the psychiatrists. He did not consider the psychiatrists to be natural leaders, managers or interested in the future of their services 'in any developmental sense'; indeed, he believed they primarily wanted to keep the *status quo* and for these reasons Richard believed they perceived the strategy to be a 'dilution of beds'. In short, Richard argued, 'they felt threatened, acted like children and ran away with the ball'.

Another possible reason for the difficulties, he suggested, was his desire to establish himself in the new general management role. His 'newness' to the health service meant his 'vision' of the strategy was poorly defined. He admitted that his own understanding of his object-ives in making the change had grown as he was forced to justify the strategy to others and his enthusiasm for the project had at times overridden his judgement. Richard did not feel that the location of consultants' contracts at the region had hindered the progress of the strategy, or would have influenced the way in which he had chosen to involve the consultants in this particular initiative.

Why Change was Difficult – Other Managers' Views

Informants were divided in their praise and criticism of the strategy itself, the DGM's role in its formation and the consultation process. Those who were complimentary about each of these issues also saw the problems lying with the attitude and obstinacy of the psychiatrists. A number of quotations illustrate this personality-based view of why change was slow:

> You will find they say 'yes' to everything you have to offer if it's going to occur ten years hence. When they realised it was going to happen they did a U-turn. (UGM-community)

> They are impossible people to deal with, they are not a cohesive group but kick one and they all limp. (District Treasurer)

> They were on board when it was conceptual – they put their heads together and worked out the ramifications and it frightened them. (The Chair)

Many of the management team, however, were at least partially aware of the importance of some social processes; for example, some thought the psychiatrists felt threatened because the strategy, with its emphasis on the community care, served to erode their traditional base of hospital beds. An additional threat was seen to be the enhancement of the status of other professions relative to their own:

> We were expecting the psychiatrists to agree a new policy that will make them redundant...we were, in fact, abandoning the medical model. (UGM-community)

The DGM was criticized by most of his managerial colleagues for his failure to gain the commitment of his senior managers to the strategy. One informant claimed the district management board members collectively were never overtly asked their opinion, yet many had deeply-held concerns about the viability of community care as an option for the NHS. The UGM for the acute unit said:

> It was never actually discussed as a proper item in the management board and certainly not in terms of 'what do you think? what can we do?' It was brought to us as 'what we have done'.

Managers also highlighted poor advice to the DGM as one reason for the problems. Some managers spoke of his failure to know where the real flow of information in the system was because he was a newcomer to the NHS. For example, Richard was criticized for believing the chair of the division represented the views of the psychiatrists' and only listening to the DNS.

Several informants spoke of the 'unnerving' pace at which the strategy was pursued as a reason for its limited success:

> Members were overwhelmed by the pace and were always worried about it.   (The Chair)

> Because of the pace, not all the psychiatrists were consulted... Management was almost saying they knew more about what was required than the psychiatrists.   (Consultant psychiatrist)

Several were critical of the fragmentation of the 'core group' which meant the strategy itself became fragmented:

> The strategy was written to satisfy too many people. The ideas were good individual ideas but there were too many people who felt it was their responsibility, so no-one was in charge.

Finally the confidence placed by Richard in the DNS was given by other managers interviewed as an explanation for the problems experienced. The DNS was thought to have a similar character and managerial approach to Richard, 'a lateral thinker, a bit impetuous and adopted an attitude of we must get it through at any cost'. Such similarities were thought to blind them to each other's faults.

Why Change was Difficult – The Consultant Pychiatrists' Views

The five consultants who were interviewed were, in the main, critical of the rationale behind the strategy, and two felt the word 'strategy' to be a misnomer. This group of consultants felt that the medical viewpoint was drowned out by the paramedical and nursing staff and members from social services.

The psychiatrists were asked to comment on the role of the general manager and the general management process with respect to the strategy. All responses echoed the following quotation:

> It appeared to be democratic, but, on the whole, management made decisions and in this respect it [the strategy] appeared dictatorial.

Most comments echoed the statement of one psychiatrist:

> The DGM means well, but he does not know what his junior management colleagues are doing. [They were particularly critical of the UGM Community]. We take part in meetings and discuss things, but the final decisions are made by the so-called managers and not by the clinicians who, in many respects, know best.

However, the consensus view from psychiatrists was that they did not want to play a managerial role in the NHS. The following quotations capture this point:

> Doctors would probably prefer to go on 'doctoring' if they felt they could trust managers. Trust is the big issue – if that was there, we would be happy merely advising.

> The clinicians' time is very valuable and shouldn't be used for administrative purposes.

In short, the psychiatrists as a group felt that the strategy had not been successful:

> We don't have a strategy. You cannot call resettlement of a few patients from the mental hospitals, a mental health strategy.

Many of these explanations were notable for their individualistic or personality-centred character – for example the 'difficult personalities' of the psychiatrists, or the alleged stubbornness or ineffectiveness of particular managers – and for the fact that they frequently indicated only a very limited understanding of the way in which people's actions were constrained by broader social processes. In other words, most players were too involved in the game – that is, the political struggle – to take what Elias (1987, pp.105–6) called a detour *via* detachment, to stand back and to analyse their own and other people's actions, not from their own relatively involved perspective but from a relatively detached position. Within the heat of the immediate struggle it is, of course, not easy to stand back and try to develop such a relatively detached view, though it is worth noting that those managers who are able to do so will almost certainly encounter fewer problems and will also enhance their chances of achieving rather more of their stated goals.

A further implication of the above is that those studies of health care management which have as their main source of data what individual managers say about health care management are seriously flawed. Views such as those expressed by the DGM in the study – that change was hard to achieve largely because of the obstinate personalities of the psychiatrists – should be treated not as an explanation, but as data to be explained. Quite clearly, if players such as our DGM had an adequate understanding of processes of organizational change, there would be no need for sociological analysis. Data which take the form of the relatively involved perceptions of participants need to be complemented, not just by accounts from other key players, but also by a relatively detached examination of the complex figurations in which all these people work.

The policy process involves many people at different levels within and outside the organization, and the extent to which different groups are committed to or opposed to the prevailing policy, and the strategies which they adopt in relation to that policy, play an important part in determining its outcome. However, the perspectives of the players in relation to these issues should be treated not as detailed analyses, but as more or less involved expressions of their own perceived interests. A properly sociological analysis should, therefore, seek to explain those perspectives in terms of the players' specific positions within the figuration of relationships amongst those involved in the policy process.

7 Conclusion

THE BOOK REVISITED

The meat of this book can be found in Chapter 4, where a comprehensive review of the Griffiths Report which prompted the third reorganization of the NHS was given. This Report was an attempt to shift the culture of the NHS from an administrative culture to that of a managerial culture. General managers were to be the key change agents in this respect. It was they who were ultimately responsible for attempting to improve quality, ensure value for money, provide a customer-focused service and encourage professionals to play a part in the management of their service. The Griffiths Report is remarkable in the sense that, despite its brevity, it caused a sensation in the NHS. It raised many heartfelt concerns for those working in the NHS and was yet another change for them to adjust to, coming so soon after the 1982 reorganization.

The Report made a number of important assumptions. These included:

- politicians will deliver clear policies which general managers will implement;
- general management will not challenge existing arrangements for accountability;
- private industry is more effectively managed than the public sector;
- it is possible to transfer approaches employed in business management to the management of the NHS;
- the democratic nature of the NHS leads to poor management;
- the general manager can be the final decision-taker and manage the considerable power of professional groups in the NHS;
- output/outcome measurement is straightforward in the NHS and the NHS consists solely of hospital services.

The discussion of these assumptions in Chapter 4 is not meant to convey political carping, but merely to illustrate the points of debate that might have been taken up following the publication of the Report, yet rarely were these points debated in the commentary and furore which followed its publication. Furthermore, it was argued that a team of highly-regarded and highly-competent business people could not be expected to get to grips with the complexities of the NHS in the time allowed by government. In short, the constraints on the members of the Griffiths team and, in particular, the pressure on the team to come up with a quick diagnosis of the problems of the NHS, made it difficult for the team to take time in reaching their conclusions, to reflect and to consider calmly, in short, to take what Elias called a detour *via* detachment.

Policies such as those arising from the Griffiths Report are not born in a vacuum, but emerge out of existing relationships and policies. Chapter 2 attempted to explore these issues. Specifically, Chapter 2 drew on historical data documenting the formation of the NHS, the pressures to reorganize and details of the two reorganizations. This chapter revealed the growing complexity of the organization of the NHS, as well as the increasing interdependence of groups involved in delivering health services. The largely ethnographic studies of local health services pre-1983 proved extremely helpful in highlighting the complexities of delivering health services. They consistently question the rationalistic assumptions of the essentially bureaucratic reorganizations of 1974 and 1982. The more general conclusions of these studies include the following:

- those working in local health care systems can, and do, circumvent national policies;
- decisions affecting local health care delivery evolve in bargaining situations and, although policy processes at local level are incremental and plural, the distribution of power is weighted towards the medical profession;
- there is genuine uncertainty amongst health service managers as to how to prioritize the many demands on finite resources;
- managerial behaviour is problem-driven rather than objective-driven;
- there seems to have been great reluctance amongst those managing health services to question the value of existing patterns of service or to propose major changes in them; and finally
- managers seem to behave as if other groups of employees, rather than the public, were the clients of the health service.

These are extremely useful points for those undertaking research in the area of health services management. Interestingly, the fruits of this body of research have rarely informed policy discussions.

Nonetheless, it was argued initially in Chapter 2 that a weakness of the existing research on health services management is that studies do not adequately locate managers' actions in the wider social context – that is, in the complex network of relationships of which managers are a part. Indeed, quite often the complexity of these networks is reduced such that managerial relationships are seen as involving only those people with whom the managers or management team have face-to-face contact.

In addition, this body of research has generally ignored the impact of health services management on patient care and health. The tendency for researchers to concentrate on face-to-face relationships is not surprising for it reflects the tendency, particularly in western societies, to think of relationships in largely individualistic terms and also reflects the fact that in the course of development of most western societies, people have come to experience themselves increasingly strongly as separate beings, distinct from other people.

The book's central objective was to explore the possibility of applying some of Norbert Elias's ideas to the study of health care organizations and management. It has been argued that this is a fruitful framework which allows researchers to consider the actions of managers within the social context of which they are a part, thus overcoming some of the weaknesses of previous research on health services management. The main principles of figurational or process sociology, an approach pioneered by Elias, were outlined in Chapter 3. Specifically, four themes of Elias's work were considered to be particularly helpful.

Firstly, Elias highlights the importance of viewing sociology as the study of people in the plural. Human beings are interdependent with each other in a variety of ways and their lives evolve in, and are significantly shaped by, the social figurations they form together. Figuration refers simultaneously to acting human beings and their interdependence. Secondly, Elias notes that figurations are constantly in flux, undergoing changes of different kinds. It is therefore critical that researchers pay attention to how relationships have come to be and in this sense a figurational approach is necessarily a developmental approach. Thirdly, many of the long-term developments taking place in human figurations have been, and continue to be, largely unplanned or unforeseen and it is in this context that Elias referred to 'blind' social processes. It is the unintended outcomes flowing from complex human interactions which make a sociological perspective imperative. Finally, central to Elias's concept of figuration

is the concept of power chances or balance of power, for while everyone is involved in networks of interdependency, not all people are
equally interdependent. The more dependent individuals are on
others, the less power chances they have and *vice versa*. However, it
is important to note that even the most powerful groups are never all-
powerful, for they are inevitably dependent to some degree on other
less powerful groups.

The empirical material presented sought to explore the figuration of
which the newly appointed district general managers were a part and,
in particular, how people within this figuration were bonded to each
other. A striking feature of the way in which DGMs worked in the
second, third and fourth years of the job was how much time they
spent dealing with district management issues (this implies the centrality of the relationship between district directors and UGMs, and
the role of these people in relation to strategy or managing operations)
and dealing with issues generated by the Centre, often elaborated
through region. Less time was spent on issues to do with the DHA
which is, of course, the main vehicle designed to ensure that local
health services were accountable to the local community. Significantly
more time was spent on the relationships with doctors (in terms of
dealing with the consequences of doctors' activities) than those involving nurses or with the array of community groups associated with
local health services.

Chapter 5 presented a great deal of largely descriptive data focusing
on these relationships and the efforts the sample DGMs made to
improve the quality of the local health services. There appear to
have been a number of unplanned and unanticipated outcomes of
the implementation of the Griffiths proposals, and in some cases,
those outcomes were the very reverse of the objectives set out in the
Griffiths Report. There outcomes included the following:

1. There appears to have been a trend towards greater centralization
    of power within the health service, accompanied by increased
    bureaucracy, a proliferation of policy objectives and a shrinkage
    of resources, all of which served to curtail the freedom of the
    district to meet the needs of its local population.
2. There seems to be more, rather than less, confusion in terms of
    accountability structures in the NHS. At the beginning of their
    appointments, general managers were extremely clear that they
    were accountable to their DHA and, through them, to the
    community. The data presented suggest that in practice, three

channels of accountability weighed heavily on the DGMs: (a) The Secretary of State, regional chair and district chair; (b) DHSS, RHA, DHAs; and (c) The management board and RGM. These three channels combined to obscure general managers' accountability to the public and also led them to play down, in relative terms, the importance of nurses, trade unions and other local groups.

3. Within districts, very different models existed of district/unit relationships. DGMs differed in their views of their leadership role and the place of professional advice in the implementation of the general management change agenda.

4. The status and power of the nursing profession appears to have declined. Nurses were often given quality assurance roles which were frequently seen as 'non'-jobs, and this reduced their credibility in shaping policy decisions.

5. Because general management was introduced at a time when the government, led by Margaret Thatcher, was seeking dramatically to reduce public expenditure, general management and cuts became inextricably linked such that notions of improving the management process were greeted cynically.

6. Doctors, as an established and powerful group in the NHS, united against the introduction of general management and saw it as a tool of government to undermine the NHS. They did not flock to take up general management posts as government had hoped and were deeply suspicious of general management as a vehicle to improve health services. They did not see themselves as 'natural managers' as Griffiths believed would be the case.

7. Improvements in quality mainly took the form of improvements in hotel services, rather than improvements in the quality of medical care. In part, this was because improvements in the former did not involve managers in challenging the power of clinicians, and, in part, it was because improvements in the former were easier to measure and could be taken as an indication of managerial 'success'.

8. More or less independent groups within the NHS become more interdependent. This situation occurred partly as a result of a general management system replacing the old functional professional hierarchies and partly because static resources, numerous new priorities for health care, an increase in monitoring and poor information meant there had to be more dialogue between groups if a health service was to be provided at all.

The question then arises of how we can account for the gap between the intentions and aspirations expressed in the Griffiths Report, and what the introduction of general management was able to deliver. The argument of most of the evaluations of general management seems to be that if only things had been organized differently and if mistakes had not been made, then general management might have been more successful. This assumes that it is possible to draw up a rationalistic organizational structure and that people will act in a rational way within that structure. It follows from this that any intention and outcome can be explained in terms of deviation from rational action, that is in terms of non-rational action, or mistakes. These mistakes may involve the failure of the government to produce clear policies, a lack of information, the failure of managers, but they all involve failure.

Furthermore, the failures or mistakes are contingencies which are not built into theoretical models of change. Figurational or process sociologists would not share these assumptions. This is not to say that figurational sociologists do not recognize that some actions may be more rational than others, but a central part of Elias's approach to understanding human behaviour is that humans are not merely cognitive animals but also emotional animals and that all our actions, without exception, involve a mixture of cognition and emotion. Some actions are based on a higher degree of cognition, others on a higher degree of emotion, but even the most cognitively-based forms of action involve emotion as well.

As an example, Elias cites the case of scientific innovation and points out that the replacement of one scientific theory by another is not simply a question of the application of cognitive processes, but involves overcoming emotional resistances too. If this is the case even for science, where intellectual and cognitive processes are stressed most explicitly and where the organizational structures which are being established have been set up to privilege cognitive and intellectual processes, then it follows that as one moves away from scientific procedures the emotive content of behaviour is likely to increase. Certainly it is the case that when approaching something as complex as organizational change, especially in an organization as complex, as multi-faceted and with as many interest groups as the NHS, no figurational sociologist would make the assumption that people will act in a wholly rational, or non-emotive, way and that mistakes will not be made.

Indeed, a fundamental assumption of 'figurationalists' in this respect would be that mistakes – things not planned for, not intended or not foreseen – are an almost inevitable consequence. In this sense, mistakes and unintended consequences are an inevitable outcome of change. They are not to be explained in terms of some deviation from a rationalistic model. Furthermore, a satisfactory model must be one that incorporates human emotion as part of the explanatory framework and conceptualizes human beings as they really are; that is, as involved emotional beings rather than as humans who have no emotions, no feelings and who are concerned simply with the application of rational procedures to the exclusion of all else.

Most people I spoke to about the introduction of general management into the NHS were most concerned about how the change affected them. Questions they asked about the implications of general management involved a high emotive content, for example: 'What does the change mean for me?'; 'What are the implications of the change in terms of how my work is being valued?'; 'Is my work being demoted?'; 'Does this mean people don't value me, don't value my work?'; 'What are the implications for my sense of self-worth?'. Thus doctors were not just defending occupational interests on a rational level, but were, in part, defending their self-image as people doing a good and worthwhile job that is being threatened by other people who do not, for example, understand the nature of clinical medicine.

Within a complex organizational structure like the NHS, there are a multiplicity of groups, some acting in a more rational, some in a less rational way, some in a more involved or less involved way, some groups with more access to information which will aid their decision-making, other groups with less access to the information they need in order to take rational decisions. There is also a variety of groups with different career interests and these involve emotive as well as cognitive elements – who will be involved in struggles. It is important to take these sorts of emotional resistances to change into account when building models of change, thus avoiding the construction of rationalistic models which can, at best, offer only a limited understanding.

One of the objectives in this book has been to set out an approach which, I believe, more adequately theorizes than do existing approaches what is a common aspect of managed change, namely unplanned outcomes. Throughout the book, the complex interweaving of planned and unplanned processes has been stressed, and it has been suggested that Elias's game models provide a means of temporarily isolating and focusing upon these complex processes of interweaving, thereby making them more easily understandable. However, the fact that it has been argued that processes of managed change almost inevitably have unplanned outcomes does not mean that planning is a futile process, or that the principle of planning should be opposed; indeed, the reverse is actually the case, for planning is a necessity if we are to overcome the major social problems, including the provision of adequate health care to all our citizens, which confront us in the late twentieth century.

It might be felt that a commitment to planning fits uneasily along-side what might be interpreted as a sceptical view of planning outlined in this book. However, what has been set out should be seen not as a sceptical, but as a realistic, view of planning. In this context I am acutely aware of the fact that, as Elias pointed out, our knowledge of and our ability to control 'natural' processes are considerably more developed than are our knowledge of and our ability to control social processes; and it is important – and it is perhaps especially important for those involved in the planning process – to be realistic about the limitations of our ability, within the constraints imposed by our current knowledge, to control social processes. To recognize the limits of our ability to control planning processes is not, however, to suggest that we have no control, nor does it undermine the case for planning any more than a recognition of the limited effectiveness, for example, of radiotherapy as a means of treating certain forms of cancer indicates that we should abandon radiotherapy altogether. In each case the appropriate course of action is not to abandon those strategies which currently have limited success, but rather to seek to make them more effective.

Given what has been said about unplanned outcomes, it is clearly imperative that a systematic process of monitoring should be built into all policy implementation from the outset; if we do not monitor the consequences of the implementation of policy then we can have no clear idea of the degree to which, if at all, we are achieving our policy goals and, as has been argued, it is certainly foolish to assume that a policy designed to achieve certain goals actually achieves those goals and that it does not have other consequences which may, perhaps, be the very reverse of what was intended. This may seem little more than a statement of the obvious, but commentators on change in the NHS are continually surprised by the lack of systematic monitoring which is often characteristic even of large-scale planned projects, and of the tendency, perhaps when funding becomes tight, to assume that the monitoring process can safely be cut back without any significant damage to the project. One might argue that, on the contrary, any economies which may be sought by cutting back on the monitoring process are likely to be false economies, and that monitoring should be at the very heart of policy implementation. Only by systematic monitoring can we know whether or not, or the degree to which, the policy goals are being achieved, and only then, armed with this knowledge, can we initiate appropriate remedial action.

It is dangerous, of course, to assume that such remedial action is any less problematic than the implementation of the original policy, for any remedial action is itself also likely to have unplanned outcomes. However, the recognition that this process is a complex one, and that our ability to control outcomes is limited, does not constitute a legitimate reason for abandoning the planning process. Indeed, it has been suggested that a recognition of our currently relatively limited control over social processes is, insofar as it represents a relatively detached and more adequate appraisal of the situation, a first step towards improving that control.

It is not appropriate to dwell on the latest reorganization of the NHS here, except to say that the reforms have increased the complexity of NHS management. The research agenda is large and interesting and it is hoped that some of the ideas put forward in this book will be of use to those of us attempting to contribute to ongoing debates about health care and, in particular, ensuring that debates usefully feed into the ultimate goal of health services – improving health.

Notes

2 Reorganizing the NHS: Theory and Practice

1. Klein argues that reorganization set the 'voice of the expert' into the concrete of the institutional structure, even more firmly than Bevan's design had done. Doctors (and nurses) were represented on both regional and area authorities; the profession had a complex advisory machinery which was to articulate professional opinion and the DMT gave representatives of the medical profession veto rights. Klein argues such extensive concessions should be viewed not so much as a victory for the corporate organizations of the medical profession, but as an acknowledgement of medical syndicalism (Klein, 1983, p. 95).

2. A number of studies have been carried out looking at professionals working within bureaucracies (Wilensky, 1964) and into appropriate organizational structures, enabling the utilization of professional skills. (Litwak, 1961; Scott, 1966; Etzioni, 1964). Some of this research has demonstrated that the two institutional modes can sit comfortably side-by-side and that projected role conflicts can be dealt with by individuals (Benson, 1973; Daniels, 1975). Rueschemeyer points out that more circumspect analysis of professionalization acknowledges that expert occupational groups have not been deprived of their knowledge-based discretion and autonomy at the workplace in either public or corporate employment (Rueschemeyer, 1986, p. 126). This evidence has brought into question the idea of an incipient proletarianization of knowledge-bearing occupations (Oppenheimer, 1973).

3 Eliasian Sociology

1. Except for the work of De Swaan, who is more concerned with the development of health care as part of overall welfare provision, rather than with the analysis of organizational structure *per se*.
2. *aperti* refers to openness (as in aperture) as opposed to *clausus* (closed).
3. An example quoted by Patrick Murphy in course material for the MSc Sociology of Sport and Sport Management, University of Leicester.
4. It is important to note that while the social fund of knowledge has grown rapidly in the last four or five hundred years, the problems which confront people living in the most developed societies have also become considerably more complex over that period. Thus, while our knowledge of economic processes is much greater than it was in the eighteenth century, it is the case that the structure of our economy is also much more complex than it was then and, in that respect, modern economies are more difficult to control. Much the same is true in relation to other, more obviously technically-based aspects of modern societies. Thus while developments in physics have, in important respects, increased our ability to control certain critical processes, they

153

have also given rise to new problems such as the problem of the safe disposal of nuclear waste

5. While the development of a 'protective shell' is dependent on the growth of knowledge, it is of course also dependent on a number of other processes, one of the most important of which is the accumulation of other resources such as capital which may be required to construct such 'protective shells', e.g. in the construction of reservoirs and irrigation projects to overcome problems associated with drought.

6. There have been a number of critiques of Elias's work. Although this is not the place to engage in philosophical debate, it is worth recording the flavour of the criticisms. The most frequent criticism is well articulated by Pels. He argues that Elias neglects the work of other sociologists and thus reduces the complexity of the outside intellectual world: 'Elias himself, and many of his most prominent disciples, have never been particularly concerned with what other people do, preferring to "go it alone" and wrestle with "the evidence" without stopping to ask where the other wrestlers were carrying their booty' (Pels, 1991, p. 179).

    Thus, Pels concludes, Elias himself has been homo-clausus, turning his back upon an intellectual world which would never listen to this particular stranger's voice (Pels, 1991, p. 182). Mennell gives a useful summary of the common criticisms. Briefly they include: (1) *The argument from cultural relativism.* At its most extreme, this argument calls in question whether it is valid to think in terms of development processes at all – civilizing, decivilizing or any other kind. (2) The argument from *'stateless civilizations'.* This is in effect a less extreme form of the first argument: it is simply that 'civilized' modes of behaviour and personality formation are found in societies where the conditions by which Elias explains their development in Europe – principally state monopolies of violence and advanced division of social functions – are absent. (3) *The 'permissive society' argument.* This is usually deployed by critics who, while prepared perhaps to accept Elias's picture of the civilizing of manners in Europe from the Middle Ages to the early twentieth century, nevertheless point to the 'permissive society' which has emerged since then, and argue that the civilizing process has gone into reverse and thus invalidated at least some aspects of Elias's theory. (4) *The 'barbarization' argument.* This could also be called 'the death camp' argument, for the Nazi period in Germany comes immediately to critics' minds. There are many who argue that at the very time that Elias was formulating his thesis, 'Hitler was refuting the argument on the grandest scale'. In effect, this argument is yet another variant on cultural relativism: the contention is that, whatever may be true of superficial matters like table manners, fundamental qualities like the propensity to aggression and sex drives do not change much. 'Civilized' modern men and women are as capable of violence, bloodshed and cruelty as Stone Age tribal people of New Guinea (Mennell, 1989, p. 227–30).

4 The Introduction of General Management in NHS

1. The Griffiths Report gives no objective evidence of waste and offers no comparison.
2. The main source of data was 102 face-to-face interviews and 216 telephone interviews with 20 DGMs over a period of three years. In addition, interviews were carried out with district chairs, UGMs, quality assurance managers and clinicians in 20 districts, together with direct observations of DHA and District board meetings.

5 DGMs' Priorities and Actions

1. It was fairly common practice for members to play to the gallery at DHA meetings and to make political points in public which, on occasions, undermined agreements they had made in private.
2. Individual performance reviews exacerbated fears that the DGMs, worried about an adverse personal review, were more likely to act as tools of the Centre. Individual performance reviews (IPR) were introduced in the third year of general management.
3. Most doctors referred to general managers as administrators. This was a constant source of irritation to the managers.

6 Case Study

1. The case draws on 29 interviews with actors involved in the strategy as well as interviews collected over two years with the DGM.

References

Alaszewski, A., Tether, P. and McDonnell, H. (1981) 'Another Dose of Managerialism', *Social Science and Medicine*, vol. 15, no. 1, pp. 3–15.

Alford, R.R. (1975) *Health Care Politics* (Chicago, Illinois: University of Chicago Press).

Barnard, K., Lee, K., Mills, A. and Reynolds, J. (1979) *Towards a New Rationality: A Study of Planning in the NHS* (in four volumes) (Leeds, University of Leeds, Nuffield Centre for Health Services Studies).

Barnes, B. (1982) *T.S. Kuhn and Social Science* (London: Macmillan).

Barton, K. (1984) 'Will 85 Percent Principle Work?' *Health and Social Service Journal*, 12 January.

Belbin, R.M. (1991) *Management Teams. Why They Succeed or Fail* (London: Butterworth Heinemann).

Benson, J.K. (1973) 'The Analysis of Bureaucratic – Professional Conflict: Functional versus Dialectical Approaches', *Sociological Quarterly*, vol. 14, pp. 378–9.

Bloor, M. and Horobin, G. (1974) 'Conflict and Conflict Resolution in Doctor–Patient Interactions', in C. Cox and A. Mead (eds), *Sociology of Medical Practice* (London: Tavistock).

Bosanquet, N. (ed.) (1979) *Industrial Relations in the NHS: The Search for a System* (London: King's Fund).

Brown, R.G.S. (1975) *The Management of Welfare* (London: Fontana).

Brown, R.G.S. (1979) *Reorganizing the National Health Service: A Case Study of Administrative Change* (Oxford: Blackwell & Martin Robertson).

Brown, R.G.S., Griffin, S. and Haywood, S.C. (1975) *New Bottles: Old Wine?* (Hull, University of Hull, Institute for Health Studies).

Buxton, M. and Klein, R. (1978) *Allocating Health Resources: A Commentary on the Report of the Resource Allocation Working Party*. Royal Commission on the National Health Service (Research Paper No. 3) (London: HMSO, ISBN 011 73011 2 4).

Chadwick, E. (1842) *Report on the Sanitary Conditions of the Labouring Population, England*. Local Reports Reprinted by Edinburgh University Press 1965.

Carrier, J. and Kendall, K. (1986) 'NHS Management and the Griffiths Report', in M. Brenton and C. Ungerson (eds), *The Year Book of Social Policy* (London & New York: Routledge & Kegan Paul).

Cartwright, A. and Anderson, R. (1981) *General Practice Revisited* (London: Tavistock).

Chaplin, N. (1982) Reorganization, *The Institute of Health Services Management* (London: Portland Place).

Committee of Enquiry into Allegations of Ill-Treatment of Patients and Other Irregularities at Ely Hospital, Cardiff (1969) (Chairman: Mr Geoffrey Howe) *Report*, London, HMSO.

Committee of Inquiry into Normansfield Hospital (1978) (Chairman: Mr M.D. Sherrard) *Report*, Cmnd 7357 (London: HMSO).

Cox, D. (1991) 'Health Service Management – A Sociological View: Griffiths and the Non-negotiated Order of the Hospital', in J. Gabe, M. Calnan and M. Bury (eds), *The Sociology of the Health Service* (London & New York: Routledge), pp. 89–111.

Curtis, J. (1986) 'Isn't It Difficult to Support Some of the Notions of "The Civilizing Process"? A Response to Dunning', in C.R. Rees and A.W. Miracle (eds), *Sport and Social Theory* (Champaign, Illinois: Human Kinetics Publishers), pp. 57–65.

Daniels, A.K. (1975) 'Professionalism in Formal Organizations', in J.B. McInley (ed.), *Processing People: Cases in Organizational Behaviour* (London: Holt, Rinehwt & Winston), ch. 7, pp. 303–38.

Davidman, M. (1984) *Reorganizing the National Health Service: An Evaluation of the Griffiths Report* (London: Social Organization Ltd).

Davies, C. (1983) 'Professionals in Bureaucracies: The Conflict Thesis Revisited', in R. Dingwell and P. Lewis (eds), *The Sociology of Professions* (London: Macmillan), pp. 177–194.

Davies, C. (1987) 'A Viewpoint: Things to Come: The NHS in the Next Decade', *Sociology of Health and Illness*, vol. 9, no. 3, pp. 302–17.

Day, P. and Klein, R.D. (1983) 'The Mobilisation of Consent Versus the Management of Conflict: Decoding the Griffiths Report', *British Medical Journal*, no. 1287, pp. 1813–15.

De Swaan, A. (1988) *In Care of the State* (Cambridge: Policy Press).

De Swann, A. (1990) *The Management of Normality. Critical Essays on Health and Welfare* (London & New York: Routledge).

Department of Health and Social Security (DHSS) (1970) *The Future Structure of the National Health Service* (London: HMSO).

Department of Health and Social Security (1971) *National Health Service Reorganisation: Consultative Document* (London: DHSS).

Department of Health and Social Security (1972a) *Management Arrangements for the Reorganised National Health Service* (London: HMSO).

Department of Health and Social Security (1972b) *National Health Service Reorganisation: England*, Cmnd 5055 (London: HMSO).

Department of Health and Social Security (1974) *Democracy in the National Health Service* (London: HMSO).

Department of Health and Social Security (1976) *Priorities for Health and Social Services in England* (London: HMSO).

Department of Health and Social Security (1983) Management Inquiry (The Griffiths Report) (London: HMSO).

Department of Health and Social Security and Welsh Office (1969). Central Health Services Council, *The Functions of the District General Hospital.* Report of the Committee (Chairman, Sir Desmond Bonham-Carter) (London: HMSO).

Department of Health and Social Security and Welsh Office (1979) *Patients First*, December (London: HMSO).

DHSS Circular (HRC(73)3 (1973) *Management Arrangements for the Reorganised NHS*, January (London: DHSS).

DHSS Circular HC(80)8 (1980) *Health Services Development: Structure and Management*, July (London: DHSS).

DHSS Circular HC(84)13 (1983) *Letter to Health Authority Chairmen* 18 November.

Dingwall, R. (1976) *Aspects of Illness* (London: Martin Robertson).

Dopson, S. (1994) 'Managing Ambiguity. A Study of the Introduction of General Management in the NHS', PhD, Leicester University.

Dopson, S. and Fitzpatrick, R. (1990) *The Manager and the Wider World* (Milton Keynes: Open University Press).

Dopson, S. and Waddington, I. (1996), 'Managing Social Change: A Process-Sociological Approach to Understanding Organisational Change Within the National Health Service', *Sociology of Health and Illness*, vol. 18, no. 4, pp. 525–50.

Doyal, L. (1980) *The Political Economy of Health* (London: Pluto Press).

Draper, P., Grenholm, G. and Best G. (1976) 'The Organization of Health Care: A Critical View of the 1974 Reorganization of the National Health Service', in D. Tucket (ed.), *Introduction to Medical Sociology* (London: Tavistock), pp. 254–90.

Dunning, E. and Sheard, K. (1976) 'The Bi-furcation of Rugby Union and Rugby League: A Case Study of Organizational Conflict and Change', *International Review of Sports Sociology*, vol. 2, no. 11, pp. 31–72.

Durkheim, E. (1938) *The Rules of Sociological Method* (New York: The Free Press).

Eckstein, H. (1958) *English Health Service* (Cambridge, Mass: Harvard University Press).

Eckstein, H. (1960) *Pressure Group of Politics* (London: Allen & Unwin).

Elcock, H. and Haywood, S. (1980) *The Buck Stops Where? Accountability and Control in the National health Service* (Hull, University of Hull, Institute for Health Studies).

Elias, N. (1939) *The Civilizing Process, History of Manners*, Vol. 1 (Oxford: Basil Blackwell).

Elias, N. (1950) 'Studies in the Genesis of the Naval Profession', *British Journal of Sociology*, vol. 1, no. 4, pp. 291–309.

Elias, N. (1956) 'Problems of Involvement and Detachment', *British Journal of Sociology*, vol. 7, no. 3, pp. 226–52.

Elias, N. (1969) 'Sociology and Psychiatry', in S.H. Foulkes and G. Steward Prince (eds), *Psychiatry in a Changing Society* (London: Tavistock), pp. 117–44.

Elias, N. (1970) *What is Sociology?* (London: Hutchinson).

Elias, N. (1971) 'Sociology of Knowledge: New Perspectives', *Sociology*, vol. 5, no. 2, pp. 149–68, and no. 3, pp. 355–70.

Elias N. (1977) 'Zur Grundlegung einer Theorie sozialer Prozesse), *Zeitschrift fur Soziologie*, vol. 6, no. 2, 127–49.

Elias, N. (1982) *The Civilizing Process, State Formation and Civilization*, Vol. 2 (Oxford: Basil Blackwell).

Elias, N. (1987) *Involvement and Detachment* (Oxford: Basil Blackwell).

Elias, N. and Scotson, J.L. (1965) *The Established and the Outsiders: A Sociological Enquiry into Community Problems* (London: Frank Cass).

Eskin, F. and Newton, P. (1977) 'A Survey of Public Knowledge in Relation to the National Health Service Reorganization', *Community Health*, vol. 9, no. 2, pp. 114–19.

Etzioni, A. (1964) *Modern Organizations*. (Englewood Cliffs, NJ: Prentice-Hall).

Fayol, H. (1949) *General and Industrial Management* (London: Pitman).

Flynn, A., Gray, A., Jenkins, W., Rutherford, B. and Plowden, W. (1988) 'Accountable Management in British Central Government: Some Reflections on the Official Record', *Financial Accountability in Management*, vol. 4, no. 3, Autumn.

Foot, M. (1973) *Aneurin Bevan*, Vol. 2. (London: Davies–Poynter).

Forsyth, G. (1966) *Doctors and State Medicine: A Study of the British National Health Service* (London: Pitman Medical).

Forte, P.G.L. (1986) *Decision-Making and Planning in a District Health Authority: A Review and a Case Study*: Working Paper no. 466 (Leeds: University of Leeds School of Geography).

Foucault, M. (1973) *The Birth of the Clinic* (London: Tavistock).

Glenerster, H., Korman, N. and Marslen-Wilson, F. (1983) 'Plans and Practice: The Participants' Views', *Public Administration*, vol. 61, no. 3, pp. 253–64.

Goudsblom, J. (1977) 'Responses to Norbert Elias's Work in England, Germany, the Netherlands and France', in P.R. Gleichmann (ed.), *Human Figurations* (Amsterdams Sociologisch Tijdschnjt), pp. 37–97.

Gouldner, A.W. (1973) *For Sociology* (London: Alan Lane).

Great Britain, Ministry of Health (1956) *Report of the Committee of Enquiry into the Costs of the NHS* (Chairman, C.W. Guillebaud). Cmnd 9663, (London: HMSO).

Griffiths Report (1983) *see* DHSS (1983).

Griffiths, R. (1991) *Seven Years of Progress – General Management in the NHS*. Management Lectures, Audit Commission, No. 3, June 12.

Hallas, J. (1976) 'New Structures for Old', in K. Barnard and K. Lee (eds.), *NHS Organization Issues and Prospects* (Nuffield Centre for Health Studies) pp. 27–41.

Hallas, J. (1976) *CHCs in Action* (London: Nuffield Provincial Hospitals Trust).

Ham, C. (1980) 'Community Health Council Participation in the NHS Planning System', *Social Policy Administration*, vol. 14, no. 3, Autumn, pp. 221–31.

Ham, C. (1981) *Policy-making in the National Health Service* (London: Macmillan).

Ham, C. (1982) *Health Policy in Britain* (London: Macmillan).

Ham, C. (1986) *Managing Health Services: Health Authority Members in Search of a Role* (Bristol: University of Bristol School for Advanced Urban Studies).

Handy, C. (1989) *The Age of Unreason* (London: Business Books).

Hanson, N.R. (1975) *Patterns of Discovery* (Cambridge University).

Hardy, C. (1986) 'Management in the NHS: Using Politics Effectively', *Public Policy and Administration*, vol. 1, no. 1, pp. 1–17.

Harrison, S. (1981) 'The Politics of Health Manpower' in A.F. Long and G. Mercer (eds), *Manpower Planning in the National Health Service* (Farnborough: Gower Press).

Harrison, S. (1982) 'Consensus Decision-making in the National Health Service: A Review', *Journal of Management Studies*, vol. 19, no. 4, pp. 377–94.

Harrison, S. (1988) *Managing the National Health Service: Shifting the Frontier?* (London: Chapman & Hall).

Harrison, S. (1988a) 'The Closed Shop and the National Health Service: a Case Study in Public Sector Labour Relations', *Journal of Social Policy*, vol. 17, pt 1, pp. 61–81.

Harrison, S., Haywood, S. and Fussell, C. (1984) 'Problems and Solutions: The Perceptions of NHS Managers', *Hospital and Health Services Review*, vol. 80, no. 4.

Harrison, S., Hunter, D.J., Marnoch, G. and Pollitt, C. (1989) *General Management in the National Health Service: Before and After The White Paper.* Nuffield Institute Reports, No. 2, August.

Harrison, S., Hunter, D.J. and Pollitt, C. (1990) *The Dynamics of British Health Policy* (London: Unwin Hyman).

Harrison, S., Hunter, D., Marnoch, G. and Pollitt, C. (1992) *Just Managing: Power and Culture in the National Health Service* (London: Macmillan).

Hayek, F.A. (1945) 'The Use of Knowledge in Society', *American Economic Review*, vol. 35, no. 4, pp. 519–30.

Haywood, S.C. (1977) *Decision Making in the New NHS: Consensus or Constipation?* (London: King's Fund Project Paper, No. 17).

Haywood, S.C. (1979) 'Team Management in the NHS: What is it all About?', *Health and Social Service Journal*, Centre 8 Paper, 5 October.

Haywood, S. (1983) *District Health Authorities in Action* (Research Report No. 19) (Birmingham: University of Birmingham Health Services Management Centre).

Haywood, S. and Alaszewski, A. (1980) *Crisis in the National Health Service* (London: Croom Helm).

Haywood, S. and Alaszewski, A. (1983) *The National Health Service: Who Rules?* (London: Croom Helm).

Haywood, S.C., Alaszewski, A., Elcock, H.J., James, T.L. and Law, E. (1979) *The Curate's Egg...Good in Parts: Senior Officer Reflections on the NHS* (Hull, University of Hull, Institute for Health Studies).

Haywood, S. and Ranade, W. (1985) *District Health Authorities in Action: Two Years On* (Birmingham: University of Birmingham Health Services Management Centre).

Hunter, D.J. (1979a) 'Coping with Uncertainty, Decisions and Resources Within Health Authorities', *Sociology of Health and Illness*, vol. 1, no. 1, pp. 41–67.

Hunter, D.J. (1979b) 'Practice, decisions and resources in the National Health Service, Scotland', in K.M. Boyd (ed.), *The Ethics of Resource Allocation* (Edinburgh: Edinburgh University Press).

Hunter, D.J. (1979c), 'Decisions and Resources in the NHS in Scotland', Ph.D thesis, University of Edinburgh.

Hunter, D.J. (1980) *Coping with Uncertainty* (Letchworth: Research Studies Press).

Hunter, D.M. (1984) 'Managing Health Care', *Social Policy and Administration*, vol. 18, no. 1, pp. 41–67.

Hunter, D.J. (1986) *Managing the National Health Service in Scotland: Review and Assessment of Research Needs.* Scottish Health Services, Study No. 45 (Edinburgh: Scottish Home and Health Department).

Hunter, D.J. (1988) 'The Impact of Research on Restructuring the British National Health Service', *The Journal of Health Administration Education*, vol. 6, vo. 3, pp. 537–53.

Hunter, D.J., Harrison, S., Marnoch, G. and Pollitt, C. (1988) *For Better or Worse? Assessing the Impact of General Management on the NHS*. Paper presented at ESRC Conference, 7 July.

Illich, I. (1975) *Limits to Medicine* (London: Marion Boyars).

Jamous, H. and Peloille, B. (1970) 'Professions or Self-Perpetuating Systems: Changes in the French University-Hospital System', in J.A. Jackson (ed.), *Professions and Professionalisation* (Cambridge: Cambridge University Press).

Jeffrey, M. and Sachs, H. (1983) *Rethinking General Practice: Dilemmas in Primary Medical Care* (London: Tavistock).

Jewson, N. (1974) 'Medical Knowledge and the Patronage System in Eighteenth Century England', *Sociology*, vol. 8, pp. 369–85.

Johnson, M. (1976) 'Whose Stranger Am I? or Patients Really are People', in K. Barnard and K. Lee (eds), *NHS Reorganization Issues and Prospects*. The Nuffield Centre for Health Studies, pp. 80–94.

Johnson, T. (1972) *Professions and Power* (London: Macmillan).

Killminster, R. (1991) 'Evaluating Elias', *Theory, Culture and Society*, vol. 8, pp. 165–76.

Kingston, W. and Rowbottom, R. (1989) *Making General Management Work in the NHS. A Guide to General Management for NHS Managers (Sigma Centre: Brunel University)*.

Klein, R. (1983) *Politics of the National Health Service* (London: Longman).

Klein, R. (1984a) 'The Politics of Ideology Versus the Reality of Politics: The Case of Britain's NHS in the 1980s', *Milbank Fund Quarterly Health and Society*, pp. 6211–217.

Klein, R. (1984b) 'Who Makes the Decisions in the NHS?', *British Medical Journal*, vol. 2, no. 88, 2 June, pp. 1706–8.

Klein, R.E. and Lewis, J. (1976) *The Politics of Consumer Representation: A Study of Community Health Councils* (London: Centre for Studies in Social Policy).

Kogan, M., Goodwin, B., Henkel, M., Korman, M., Packwood, T., Bush, A., Hoyes, V., Ash, L. and Tester, J. *et al.* (1978) *The Working of the National Health Service*, Royal Commission on the National Health Service, Research Paper No. 1 (London: HMSO).

Kranendonk, W. (1989) *Society as Process. A Bibliography of Figurational Sociology in the Netherlands* (University of Amsterdam).

Lakatos, I. and Musgrave, A.E. (1970) *Criticism and the Growth of Knowledge* (Cambridge University Press).

Larkin, G. (1988) 'Medical Dominance in Britain: Image and Historical Reality', *The Milbank Quarterly*, vol. 66, suppl. 2, pp. 117–32.

Larson, M.S. (1977) *The Rise of Professionalism: A Sociological Analysis* (Berkeley, Los Angeles and London: University of California Press).

Lee, K. and Mills, A. (1982) *Policy-Making and Planning in the Health Sector* (London: Croom Helm).

Legge, K. (1984) *Evaluating Planned Organizational Change* (London: Academic Press).

LeGrand, J. (1980) *The Strategy of Equality* (London: Allen & Unwin).

Levitt, R. and Wall, A. (1989) *Reorganized National Health Service*, 3rd edn (London: Chapman & Hall).

Litwak, E. (1961) 'Models of Bureaucracy Which Permit Conflict', *American Journal of Sociology*, vol. 67.

Mastenbroek, W.F.G. (1987) *Conflict Management and Organizational Development* (Chichester: John Wiley).

McKeown, T. (1976) *The Role of Medicine*. Nuffield Provincial Hospitals Trust.

McNulty, T.H. (1989) *Organizations, Culture and the Management of Change in the NHS*. Ph.D Thesis, University of Warwick.

Medawar, P. (1969) *Induction and Intuition in Scientific Thoughts* (London: Methuen).

Medical Services Review Committee (1962) *A Review of the Medical Services in Great Britain* (Chairman, Sir A. Porritt) (London: Social Assay).

Mennell, S. (1989) *Elias, N. Civilization and the Human Self-Image* (Oxford: Basil Blackwell).

Merton, R.K. (1936) 'The Unanticipated Consequences of Purposive Social Action', *American Sociological Review*, vol. 1, no. 6, pp. 894–904.

Merton, R.K. (1949) *Social Theory and Social Structure* (Geeneve: Press)

Ministry of Health (1944) *A National Health Service*. Cmd 6502 (London: HMSO).

Ministry of Health (1956) *Report of the Committee of Enquiry into the Cost of the National Health Service* (Chairman C.W. Guillebaud). Cmnd 9663 (London: HMSO).

Ministry of Health (1959) *Report of the Maternity Services Committee* (Chairman, Earl of Cranbrook) (London: HMSO).

Ministry of Health (1963), Central Health Services Council, Standing Medical Advisory Committee, *Fieldwork of the Family Doctor* (Chairman, Dr A. Gillie) (London: HMSO).

Ministry of Health (1967) *First Report of the Joint Working Party on the Organization of Medical Work in Hospitals* (Chairman, Sir G. Godber) (London: HMSO).

Ministry of Health (1968) *The Administrative Structure of Medical and Related Services in England and Wales* (London: HMSO).

Ministry of Health and Scottish Home and Health Department (1966) *Report of the Committee on Senior Nursing Staff Structure* (Chairman, B. Salmon) (London: HMSO).

Morgan, M., Calnan, M. and Manning, M. (1985) *Sociological Approaches to Health and Medicine* (London: Croom Helm).

Navarro, V. (1976) *Medicine under Capitalism* (New York: Prodist).

Oppenheimer, N. (1973) 'The Prolaterization of the Professional. Professionalization and Social Change', *Sociological Review*, monograph 20.

Parsons, T. (1951) *The Social System* (London: Routledge).

Parsons, T. (1961) 'Suggestions for a Sociological Approach to the Theory of Organizations', in A. Etzioni (ed.), *Complex Organizations: A Sociological Reader* (New York: Holt, Rinehart & Wimta).

Pels, R. (1991) 'Elias and the Politics of Theory', *Theory, Culture and Society*, vol. 8, pp. 77–183.

Perry, J.L. and Kramer, K.L. (1983) *Public Management: Private and Public Perspectives* (California: Mayfield Press).

Petchey, R. (1986) 'The Griffiths Reorganization of the NHS: Fowlerism by Stealth?', *Critical Social Policy*, vol. 17, pp. 87–101.

Peters, T. and Waterman, R. (1982) *In Search of Excellence: Lessons from America's Best-Run Companies* (New York: Harper & Row).

Pettigrew, A., Ferlie, E. and McKee, L. (1992) *Shaping Strategic Change* (London: Sage).

Pill, R. and Stott, N.C.M. (1982) 'Concepts of Illness Causation and Responsibility: Some Preliminary Data from a Sample of Working Class Mothers', *Social Science and Medicine*, vol. 16, pp.13–51.

Pollitt, C. (1990) *Managerialism and the Public Services: The Anglo-American Experience* (Oxford: Blackwell).

Popper, K. (1968) *The Logic of Scientific Discovery* (Lava: Hutchinson).

Powles, J. (1973) 'On Limitations of Modern Medicine', *Science, Medicine and Man*, pp. 1–30.

Rathwell, T.A. (1987) *Strategic Planning in the Health Sector* (London: Croom Helm).

Report of the Committee on Local Authority and Allied Personal Social Services (1968) (Chairman, F. Seebohm) Cmnd 3703 (London: HMSO).

Report of the Royal Commission on Local Government in England (1966–1969) (Chairman, Lord Redcliffe-Maud). Cmnd 4040 (London: HMSO).

Robinson, J., Strong, P. and Elkan, R. (1989) *Griffiths ana the Nurses: National Survey of CNAs* (Nursing Policy Study Centre, University of Warwick).

Rogaly, J. (1973) *The Financial Times*, 23 January.

Royal Commission on the National Health Service (1979) Cmnd 7615 (London: HMSO).

Rowbottom, R.W., Balle, J., Cang, S., Dixon, M., Jaques, E., Packwood, T. and Tolliday, H. (1973) *Hospital Organisation* (London: Heinemann).

Rueschemeyer, D. (1986) *Power and the Division of Labour* (Quality Press).

Russell (1984) 'A Score of MPs Debate Griffiths', *British Medical Journal*, vol. 288, 19 May, p. 1546.

Schulz, R.I. and Harrison, S. (1983) *Teams and Top Managers in the NHS: A Survey and a Strategy*. Project Paper No. 41 (London: King's Fund).

Scott, W.R. (1966) 'Professionals and Bureaucracies: Areas of Conflict', in H. Vollmer and D. Mills (eds), *Professionalization* (Englewood Cliffs, N.J.: Prentice-Hall).

Seifert, R. (1992) *Industrial Relations in the NHS* (London: Chapman & Hall).

Smith, Ring, P. and Perry, J.L. (1985) 'Strategic Management in Public and Private Organizatgions: Implications of Distinctive Context and Constraints', *Academy of Management Review*, vol. 10, no.2, pp. 276–186.

Social Services Committee (1984) 'First Report Sessions, 1983–84: Griffiths NHS Management Inquiry Report (HC209)' (London: HMSO).

Spurgeon, P. and Barwell, F. (1991) *Implementing Change in the NHS* (London: Chapman & Hall).

Stewart, R. (1989) *Leading in the NHS: A Practical Guide* (London: Macmillan).

Stewart, R., Dopson, S., Gabbay, J., Smith, P. and Williams, D. (1987–88) *The Templeton College Series on District General Management, April–Jan-*

uary (London: National Health Service Training Authority (NHSTA) Publications).

Stewart, R., Smith, P., Blake, J. and Wingate, P. (1980) *The District Administrator in the National Health Service* (London: King Edward's Hospital Fund).

Stimpson, G. and Webb, B. (1978) 'The Face-to-Face interaction after the consultation in D. Tucket and J. Kanferd (eds.) *Medical Sociology* (London: Tavistock).

Stocking, B. (1985) *Initiative and Inertia: Case Studies in the NHS* (The Nuffield Provincial Hospitals Trust).

Strauss, A. (1978) *Negotiations* (San Francisco: Jossey Bass).

Strauss, A., Schatzman, L., Ehrlich, P. and Sabshin, M. (1983) 'The Hospital and its Negotiated Order', in G. Salaman and K. Thomson (eds), *People and Organizations* (London: Longman).

Strong, P. and Robinson, J. (1990) *The NHS Under New Management* (Milton Keynes: Open University Press).

Szasz, T.S. and Hollender, M.H. (1956) 'A Contribution to the Philosophy of Medicine, the Basic Models of the Doctor–Patient Relationship', *Archives of Internal Medicine*, vol. 97, pp. 585–92.

Taylor, F.W. (1947) *Scientific Management* (New York: Harper & Row).

The National Health Service Act 1946 (1946) (9 and 10 Geo. 6 Chapter 81 Park I Section) (London: HMSO).

The National Health Service Reorganisation Act (1973) (Eliz. II Chapter 32) (London: HMSO).

'The NHS verdict on HC(4)13' (1984), *Health and Social Services Journal*, 14 June.

Thompson, D.J.C. (1986) *Coalition and Decision-Making Within Health Districts*, Research Report no. 23 (Birmingham: University of Birmingham, Health Services Management Centre).

Townsend, P. and Davidson, N. (eds), (1982) *Inequalities in Health: The Black Report* (London: Pelican).

Trade Union Research Unit, Ruskin College for the Confederation of Health Service Employees (1987) *The Impact of General Management and General Managers in the NHS* (London: TURU Publication).

Waddington, I. (1973) 'The Struggle to Reform the Royal College of Physicians 1767–1771. A Sociological Analysis', *Medical History*, 17 April, pp. 107–26.

Waddington, I. (1984) *The Medical Profession in the Industrial Revolution* (Dublin: Gill & Macmillan).

Wadsworth, L., Butterfield, W. and Blaney, R. (1971) *Health and Sickness: The Choice of Treatment* (London: Tavistock).

Weber (1964) *The Theory of Social and Economic Organisation* (London: Macmillan).

Webster, C. (1988) *The Health Services Since the War*, vol. 1 (London: HMSO).

Wilensky, H.L. (1964) 'The Professionalization of Everyone?' *American Journal of Sociology* vol. 70, pp. 42–6.

Willcocks, A.J. (1967) *The Creation of the National Health Service* (London: Routledge & Kegan Paul).

Williams, J., Dunning, E. and Murphy, P. (1984) *Hooligans Abroad* (London: Routledge & Kegan Paul).

Wiseman, C. (1979) 'Strategic Planning in the Scottish Health Service – A Mixed – Scanning Approach', *Long Range Planning*, vol. 12, pt 2, pp. 103–13.

Wouters, C. (1982) 'De gemoedsnist van de verzorgingsstaat', *Maand blad Geestelijke vollksgezond heid*, 37–6, pp. 599–612.

Wouters, C. (1986) 'Formalization and Informalization: Changing Tension Balances in Civilizing Processes', *Theory, Culture and Society*, vol. 3 no. 2, pp. 1–18.

Index

167